SARAH: MOTHER OF A NATION

The *Character and Charisma* series introduces us to people in the Bible and shows how their lives have much to teach us today. All the authors in the series use their communication skills to lead us through the biblical record and apply its encouragements and challenges to our lives today. Every volume contains an *Index of Life Issues* to enhance its usefulness in reference and application.

Other books in the series:

CHARACTER AND CHARISMA SERIES

Sarah
Mother of a Nation

WENDY VIRGO

KINGSWAY PUBLICATIONS
EASTBOURNE

ISBN 0 85476 832 7

Published by
KINGSWAY PUBLICATIONS
Lottbridge Drove, Eastbourne, BN23 6NT, England.
Email: books@kingsway.co.uk

Book design and production for the publishers by
Bookprint Creative Services, P.O. Box 827, BN21 3YJ, England.
Printed in Great Britain.

Contents

Introduction:
Sarah – a Prophetic Woman

Surprisingly, for someone who lived such a long time ago, Sarah has much to say to a generation living in the twenty-first century. It occurs to me that whereas role models for men and women in former centuries tended to be people who were admired for strength of character and extraordinary achievement, today our role models are often people who are emulated for very superficial reasons. Athletes, scientists, explorers, writers and artists still continue to produce great work, but the biographies that are being written, the magazine articles and television interviews, show a huge emphasis on those who have reached notoriety because of their beautiful appearance, their wealth, an album in the charts, or a liaison with someone else rich and famous. In short, that ephemeral thing called 'glamour' is an essential ingredient to make one worth following.

We would do well to direct our young men and women to biblical characters to find the sort of role models that God would have them consider: people who had faults and failings, but whose lives demonstrated faith, courage and endurance. Such people as Joshua, David, Esther and Mary, for example, were not perfect, but showed solid, stable values worth emulating. In fact we are told very specifically to 'look

to Abraham and his wife Sarah . . .' and we have examined
some of those areas that they exemplify.

But there is one area in particular that seems especially relevant. As we enter the twenty-first century, there is an
increasing sense of God calling us out of our comfort zones
and into a fast-flowing, turbulent river. The last century was
a momentous one. It began with so many traditional values
being unquestioningly upheld, little spiritual power, and low
expectations of any change or exciting development in the
church. But within a few years the Azusa Street revival in
America and the Welsh revival had pitchforked it into a new
era. Pentecostal churches spread around the world, and the
missionary movement gained new momentum. As the
century progressed, through two world wars, other events
shook the church. There were the great healing evangelists,
the Hebridean revival, and the powerful and effective evan-
gelistic ministry of Billy Graham.

In the sixties, another issue began to make the news. The
baptism of the Holy Spirit was not a new doctrine, but had
been largely ignored or forgotten by most denominations,
and even in the Pentecostal churches it had become rather
stale and stereotyped. But suddenly it broke out again
among mainline evangelical Christians. Gradually, over the
remaining decades of the century, as more and more people
were persuaded of its validity and entered into a new relationship with God through the experience of the Spirit, it
was largely accepted that this was not a quirk embraced
merely by the 'fringe' element, but was seen as mainstream
Christianity.

The pace of change has become increasingly rapid, with
many churches radically changed or at least open to charismatic elements. One of the results is a new wave of evangel-
ism, in which courses such as Alpha play a huge part.

So the church at the beginning of this century looks very

different from the one at the beginning of the last century. Proportionately less of the population in England attend on a Sunday, but it is more widely understood among Christians that church is more than formal Sunday attendance. The people who are churchgoers now are more likely to see themselves as part of a vibrant community that has power to affect the life of the streets around them. The body may be leaner, but it is healthier and stronger.

One of the marked characteristics of this church body has become the use of spiritual gifts. This is part of the fulfilment of the prophecy of Joel, which was quoted by Peter at Pentecost: 'I will pour out my Spirit on all people. Your sons and daughters will prophesy . . .' (Acts 2:17), although prophecy is only one of many charismatic gifts. But prophecy is not only something that is operated verbally by individuals. Whole communities can be described as prophetic as they declare what God is like by their life together. Also, a person can be described as prophetic as aspects of his or her life project truth about God and his ways.

In this way Sarah was prophetic and very relevant to the present age. Her life, entwined with Abraham's, was about response to progressive revelation and moving on in the purposes of God. It was about the power of God's word to produce faith. But more than that, it was not only about her and her husband, but about how the response of individuals to the call of God can affect history.

She was one of the first of an endless line of people who have dared to leave behind everything that was dear and familiar, and set out for a land that was unknown to them. They were pioneers of a new nation out of whom would come others who would hear a clear call and rise up, captivated by the vision before them, enduring hardship, misunderstanding, deprivation and disappointment, but unable to turn away because their hearts have been caught and held.

They have seen something on the horizon, misty and undefined, but enough to keep them motivated and moving.

These are days to look for more Sarahs! We need people who have heard that voice, who are willing to take that risk to leave the safe bank of the river and jump on the frail raft bobbing dangerously in the turbulent current. It looks so perilous, at times even ridiculous, to move on from where we are and what we have built. But we belong to a God who, although unchanging in his character and principles, is never static. He has not called us to be a people who will stand still. We are not to be content to sit and admire the place we have arrived in; we are urgently to push on to the next part of his plan to reach the entire globe with the gospel. While we may not necessarily move physically from where we live, we must always have movement in our hearts, ready for change, adjustment, development, growth.

If this sounds tiring, it's because it is. If it sounds restless, it's because we follow one who had nowhere to lay his head. If it sounds hard, it's because he never said it would be soft. But to stay is to forfeit the adventure. To resist the call is never to know what could have been achieved. To stagnate is never exhilarating.

What would have happened if that elderly couple had never left Ur? If they had quite legitimately said, 'Leave it to the younger ones. We have settled down here'?

We can imagine an elderly apostle, whoever he was, sitting down to write to a number of Jewish Christians. He sharpens his quill and dips it in the ink, and inscribes on the pristine parchment, 'Epistle to the Hebrews'. As he writes he thinks of many issues that need clarification. He knows they are muddled about the place of the old sacrificial system, the significance of the temple and the altar. He begins with a magnificent reminder of the wonderful deity of Christ yet fully man, and continues to explain how he has abolished the former rituals by himself being the sacrifice once for all. He goes on to show that he is also the High Priest who ever makes intercession for us, and by whom we come boldly to the throne of grace.

But he is perturbed. As he thinks of his dear Jewish brothers he wants to stir them up to greater faith. They have become somewhat sluggish! How can he inspire them? Then he hits on the idea of reminding them of their own heroes. In order to spur them on in the present, he recalls people in the past who had partial vision, who believed God and struck out, although their revelation was incomplete. In many and various ways God spoke to them through prophets and events. They endured hardship and difficulties, but kept running with the amount of light they had to guide them: such people as Abraham and Sarah, Joseph, Moses, Daniel, Gideon, Barak, David . . . the list goes on. Now, he says, in view of their persistence, energy and courage to keep running with their partial vision, let us lay aside every weight that would hold us back and run the race looking to Jesus. Full revelation has come! He is the author of our faith and the goal for them and us. They were looking for a country, a heavenly one, and though they did not receive what was promised, they were commended for their faith. Now, says the apostle, God has planned something better for us and only together with us will they be made perfect.

Sarah was one of the first links in the chain of faithful people who believed God and obeyed him, and will be gathered up by him in the final fulfilment of all those promises. She was an ordinary woman who became extraordinary: a pioneer, prophetic, the mother of a nation.

1

It All Began with Abraham

The streets of Jerusalem rang with the shouts of an excited crowd. The Roman procurator looked down at the seething crowd from the balcony of his residence, and sighed in exasperation. His litter had been jostled in the streets by the mob and almost overturned as the crowd surged towards the council chamber. He had hoped to find some peace within his own walls, but he acknowledged grimly to himself that you might as well seek solace in a lions' den as in Jerusalem!

He thought back to his predecessor, Pontius Pilate, now recalled to Rome after the death of the emperor Tiberius. Caligula was emperor now and many changes had taken place. But one thing that did not appear to have changed in this dusty corner of the empire was the volatile disposition of its inhabitants. These Jews! He could not understand them. Religion seemed to be of supreme importance to them and they were always squabbling about some interpretation of their laws.

That was what had made him think of Pontius Pilate. As Pilate was handing over to him as successor he had warned him to tread warily. In particular, he had informed him about a new sect that had arisen. Apparently there had been a lot of conflict in the city recently because of these people.

The new procurator had innocently enquired as to what was at the bottom of it and had been surprised when the older, more experienced man had seemed somewhat troubled by what he, the younger man, appraised as merely a passing incident. Pilate told him that, a year or two back, the Sanhedrin (that is the council of the religious leaders of the Jews) had become incensed by a small town rabbi called Jesus of Nazareth, who made blasphemous claims. Although this should have been easily dealt with by their own disciplinary procedures, they had insisted that the man be executed. However, they had to have Pilate's mandate to effect his death. Pilate, not convinced of the necessity of such an extreme measure, nevertheless felt cornered, and in order to keep the peace, gave them the authority to go ahead.

The new procurator had shrugged. 'So what? It was just one obscure man, a trouble-maker.'

Pilate shifted uneasily. 'Yes, I know. But there was something about him; I believe he was a good man . . .'

'You met him?'

'Yes. I still think about him sometimes. He had a way of looking at you that made you feel he knew a lot more about . . . about . . . well, everything – even what was going on in my mind! But the really strange thing was that apparently his disciples believed he would rise from the dead! Yes, yes I know, it was all very ridiculous, but I had to supply a full guard at his tomb to satisfy those wretched men who were so set on proving he was a fraud!'

The new man was impatient. 'Well surely that was the end of it! He died and was buried in a well-guarded tomb. End of story. What is there left to worry about?'

Pilate got up from his chair and paced about the room. There were piles of scrolls everywhere, and chests half-packed with quills and parchments and tablets and seals . . .

all the paraphernalia that had accumulated in his office. Tomorrow they would be taken to Caesarea and transported back to Rome. He picked his way through and stood at the balcony looking out at the Judaean hills in the gathering twilight, his fingers drumming restlessly on the balustrade. Then he turned and faced the new man.

'You see,' he said carefully, 'we can't dismiss it as easily as that. The tomb was found to be empty, and the body just . . . disappeared. Then there began to be rumours of people seeing him alive again.' He motioned with his hand as the other man began to exclaim in disbelief. 'What you or I think about it is neither here nor there. The fact is, a lot of people did believe it and still do, and that number is growing daily. There are probably thousands in Jerusalem alone by now and it has spread into other towns and villages.'

He came across the room and poked his successor firmly on the shoulder with his forefinger. 'So I am warning you, my friend, that this is an issue that won't just go away! These Jesus people are quite vocal and powerful. No doubt there will be further eruptions and disputes, and you will have to decide how to deal with them. You will find out that the Jews are a very passionate race and nothing inflames them more than to have their traditions and rules meddled with. You will have to tread carefully but decisively. As for me, I'm better off out of it!'

The new procurator had cause to remember these words many times. Now, some seven or eight years after the death of the man from Nazareth, the streets were again filled with angry Pharisees. He watched them all surging down the narrow street in the direction of the council chamber where, once again, a man was on trial having been charged with blasphemy by a crowd of incensed city elders and lawyers, who claimed that they had heard this man speak evil of God and Moses.

Stephen was well known in Jerusalem. He was one of a quickly swelling crowd who believed that Jesus of Nazareth was the Son of God, and that although he had been killed by crucifixion, he had come back to life. Stephen was greatly loved and respected among these Jesus followers. He was a man of great integrity, and spoke fluently and boldly about Jesus whom he passionately loved. He was also a man of prayer and had even prayed for sick people, who had been healed. Many were being converted to this new faith, including a number of priests. But the rest were fanatically opposed, perceiving the Jesus followers as a threat to the whole Judaistic philosophy and way of life. What the Sanhedrin hated most about Stephen was that he was a fluent debater and was constantly getting the better of them in discussions, and his superior oratory was often making them appear foolish. They determined to suppress him.

So Stephen had been arrested and charged with blasphemy and dragged before the council. There, he was accused by men who had been bribed to twist his words. One by one they jumped up and vigorously declared that he incessantly spoke against God and Moses!

At last, the high priest called Stephen forward to make his defence. A hush fell as the young man stood with calm dignity before the agitated crowd. Unhurried, unperturbed, his eyes swept the council chamber; and although his hands were bound, he seemed more in command of the situation than they. A light seemed to radiate from his face; in fact some said that the glow was so bright that it obscured his features.

There was an intense silence. The high priest deliberately punctured the tension by demanding, 'Well? Are these things so?'

In a clear commanding voice, Stephen began his defence: 'Hear me, brothers and fathers! The God of glory appeared to Abraham our father when he lived in Mesopotamia before he lived in Haran! He said, "Depart from your country and your relatives and come into the land that I will show you!" Then Abraham departed from Ur of the Chaldaeans, and settled in Haran.'

Confidently, Stephen reminded the assembled gathering of their own history – the story of a people called out from the surrounding culture by one who revealed himself as Elohim Adonai, the Lord God. Eloquently he recounted how God had desired a people for his own possession who would be his dwelling place, and lovingly submit to him, and reflect his character and his ways. He showed how they fell into slavery, but God again called them out and delivered them; then again how they lost their way, but always he drew them back because he had a purpose in mind that was huge and wonderful. God wanted them to be his house, his temple, his vehicle to express himself to the world. As he dwelt among them they would be so like him, so reflecting his character that surrounding nations would see their mercy, their purity of heart, their justice and truth and say, 'How great is their God! We would worship him too!'

So God raised up Moses, then Joshua, and David, but history kept repeating itself. He was constantly having to disentangle them from encroaching culture and idolatry, and eventually from form and legalism. He sent prophets to recall them to the purity of their first love and vision, but they stoned the prophets and turned against him. At last he sent one who was the very incarnation of himself, but they did not recognise him.

Stephen's hearers could see where this was leading! They were becoming increasingly agitated, but he did not falter. Recklessly he plunged on with no attempt to be conciliatory or to dilute his message. Suddenly the accusers became the accused. 'You men!' Stephen cried and swung round, his manacled arm stretched out, finger pointing along the packed rows. 'You are stiff-necked and uncircumcised in heart and you are always resisting the Holy Spirit! Just as they killed and persecuted the prophets so now you also have murdered the Righteous One!'

With a roar of rage they rose up in their seats, protesting and shouting, some tearing their garments. Over the turmoil his clear voice came again. 'Look!' He was gazing up towards the ceiling. 'Heaven is open! I see him now! Jesus, the Son of man at the right hand of the Father!'

It was too much. Howling with anger they surged forward like an unstoppable flood, their fingers in their ears. 'We will hear no more!' they yelled, and fell upon him and bore him away to a place outside the city, a pit full of large stones.

The Roman procurator heard the din as they clattered past his residence. Curiously he watched, and saw their faces distorted with fury as they forced their unresisting victim along to the place of execution. He was vaguely disquieted, but shrugged it off. At least this time they had not sought his involvement! Let them deal with their problems and leave him out of it, as long as it restored the peace and he was not held responsible for any rioting!

The noise faded into the distance. What he did not hear as they hurled their rocks relentlessly at Stephen was his voice, discernible above the turmoil: 'Lord Jesus, do not hold this sin against them!' Thus he died, like his Master, with mercy and forgiveness in his heart for his murderers.

*   *   *

What was it about the life and death of Stephen that aroused such hatred? Followers of Jesus always cause disruption and conflict. They do not merge into the background. They are different, called out from the normal throng. They dance to a different tune, sing another song, answer to another voice.

They don't belong; they are strangers and aliens; in the world but not of it.

As Stephen showed when he began his defence, it all began far, far back with a man called Abram. He had lived in the most advanced city of his day, but there came a time when he was called to leave it all – his friends and family and culture – and become a wanderer, seeking something that could not be embodied in stones and buildings, yet nevertheless was an eternal dwelling place.

The voice called and tugged him. He wanted to obey. But there was someone else who was also an important part of the whole vision.

Abram had a wife.

2

Leaving Ur

The sun was already high in the sky and the shadows of the camel train lay short on the sandy ground. Sarai turned and looked back. She shaded her eyes with her hand in an endeavour to make out the city on the skyline that had been her home. It seemed to shimmer in the growing heat, but she could just discern the towers and roofs and city walls. She fancied she could see the massive gate, and imagined the camels carrying merchandise, which the jostling, shouting traders unloaded, while beggars rattled their bowls and women came in and out with their waterpots, to and from the well.

Tears pricked her eyes as she imagined the bustle in the narrow streets, the noises, the smells, the familiar inconsequential things that had coloured her entire life up to now. Ur, the great city of the Chaldaeans, had been her home all her life. She loved its solidness, the massive walls rearing up enclosing the people within in a secure embrace, shutting out any threatening intruders and the wild encroaching desert not far away.

In its encircling arms lay the most sophisticated society of the known world. She knew, from the tales of travellers and merchants, that other tribal groups lived mostly in far more

19

primitive communities without the benefits that she had learned to take for granted. She knew a world of developing thought, where men watched the stars and moon and sought to understand their courses; where elegant jewellery of gold and lapis lazuli and jasper adorned the necks of beautiful women, and fine artifacts of painted pottery adorned their houses. The streets were paved and led to massively constructed temples where the gods were worshipped, not least the moon god Nannar.

Most of all, however, Ur was where her friends and family lived, and now she was leaving them all behind.

'Sarai!' Abram's voice floated back to her from the camel train as the distance widened between them. She stood forlornly between two worlds: one that held everything dear and familiar to her and one that was frighteningly new and strange. But she could not retreat now, and choking back tears she turned resolutely and ran to catch up the camel train.

Abram saw the tears on his wife's beautiful face, but said nothing, only silently helped her to remount her camel as they resumed their journey. Bleakly she looked ahead. What did the future hold? She could see nothing but rocks and thin grass and thorny bushes. Where were they going? She threw a sidelong glance at her husband's stern face. Useless to ask him! She had already done that, a thousand times. It was because of him that they now found themselves on this journey. She would never understand him. He had everything they could want in the city they had just left: friends, property, prestige, respect, interests, culture. But he and his father both had this strange urge to leave and look for something, somewhere. When she had pressed them, they were vague and unable to express exactly what it was they were looking for. The only word that was consistently spoken was 'Canaan'. That was apparently where they were headed but they did not know why. Whether it was Terah, Abram's father, who had first got the idea into his head, or whether it was Abram who had persuaded his father to abandon Ur and go there, she was unsure. Also in their company was Lot, the son of Abram's brother. So now the three men with their households were setting out together to search for it.

Abram had become obsessed with finding this Canaan place – at least that is what Sarai thought. As for her, she wished they had never even heard of it. Not that anyone consulted her! She didn't have any choice but to go along with the rest. What puzzled her most was that her husband kept talking about looking for a city, but if Ur was not a city, what was? What city could be better than this one, she wanted to know? Then he said incomprehensible things, like it was a city that had foundations. She had laughed with irritation. What city had better-laid or stronger foundations than Ur? But she was silenced by his next remark that its architect was God (which god?) and he was building it to last. She was exasperated with him and annoyed that she did not understand. He seemed to be in possession of a secret, to know something that she did not, but she was also somewhat awed that he should have such a strong desire to find this city that it outweighed every other consideration.

As they journeyed on day after day, she thought longingly of Ur, a city already ancient and steeped in traditions long before her birth, with its own language and customs. It was situated on a fertile plain watered by the great river Euphrates and in the distant past had been one of several city states that together made up the Sumerian kingdom. The Sumerians had lived a peaceful and settled existence, developing a culture that was important in laying early foundations of civilisation in architecture and writing on clay tablets.

Then these fertile lands had been invaded by tribes who swept in from the north. One of their chieftains was a powerful warlike man named Sargon, who annexed Ur to his growing empire. This Akkadian empire continued to expand until it stretched from Mesopotamia to the Mediterranean Sea.

Once again, however, the fertile crescent was invaded – this time by the Amorites from the Zagros mountains. They further developed the city, and one of their main contributions was the building of the enormous ziggurat, the great temple to the moon god Nannar, with its distinctive stepped outline, massive, huge and arrogant, etched upon the skyline, and centuries later still etched into history as the main feature of this proud city. Ur became the leading city in Mesopotamia, and was large and prosperous. A great wall encircled it, but in addition it was protected on three sides by water, for a tributary of the Euphrates ran past it and also a canal had been constructed. The river was navigable to sea-going vessels, and ships could come from the coast some hundred miles south right up to the city harbour, bringing trade with foreign lands. Thus Ur became very rich through commerce as well as in culture.

It was during this prosperous period that Abram and Sarai and their families had lived in Ur, enjoying all the undoubted benefits of a relatively sophisticated civilisation. Now as each uncomfortable day took them further and further away from it, Sarai had to learn to adapt to a nomadic way of life. They could not travel fast or far because they were taking considerable flocks and herds with them, as well as tents and utensils, and herdsmen and servants. It was no small thing for a man of substance to set out on such a venture. Slowly they wound through the valleys, up hillsides and around rocks and boulders. They tried not to stray too far from water, so their route was often meandering as they followed the course of the great river. When they found a congenial place they would stop and pitch camp, sometimes for days or weeks at a time. Abram's and Lot's herds were thriving. When they exhausted the pasture they pulled up stakes and moved on.

But however much Sarai may have regretted leaving Ur, those days were not unpleasant. They did not often encounter hostile terrain. True, the desert was not far away, with its windblown rocks and shifting sand dunes – it lay on their west side – but they sought roughly to follow the north-westerly course of the great river and to stay on its plains. The land was fertile enough to support their livestock, and they were not short of water. Sarai gradually got used to it, but it was the unsettled nature of their life, the uncertainty, that gnawed at her. Where was all this going to end? Ur had seemed so solid, so real. Now life was impermanent, unsettled. As she padded around her tent in the chill dew of early mornings, she thought nostalgically of the paved street where her former home was; of its spacious courtyard surrounded on three sides by well-appointed rooms, with cooking and washing facilities and storage space, and an upper floor for bed chambers. During hot days and cold nights, huddled under the temporary structure of the tent, she remembered longingly the thick stone walls that had kept the temperature even: cool in hot weather and retaining warmth in the cold.

At night, when they had eaten and were sitting around the embers of the fire, Terah and Lot and Abram would talk. Sarai longed to ask questions: How far was Canaan? What was it like? Did it resemble Ur in any way? What language was spoken? Who were their gods? But Terah was vague. Sarai had often wondered if his flight from Ur had been precipitated by the death of his wife. Perhaps he had felt restless and lonely and the bustle of city life had finally

held no fascination for him any more. Certainly he seemed
not to be consoled by the great Nannar. The ziggurat that
had dominated the city was somehow menacing, its huge
stones projecting a sense of unyielding strength, but she
had to admit that it was a harsh strength, not a comfort-
ing one. Perhaps the ache in his heart caused him to flee
from a place where the worship of such a god brought no
relief, no answers, but rather added to the burdens of grief.
Shrewdly Sarai noticed that now they had left Ur behind
he seemed less concerned with arriving at Canaan and
content to meander on in a north-westerly direction.

After some weeks, they found they were approaching a
sizeable town. They suspected that it was Haran, and so it
proved to be. Haran was an Akkadian word that meant
'crossroads' and was an apt name for this settlement,
which had grown up at an intersection of caravan routes
coming south from Egypt, west from the great sea and
Syria, and also from the south-east and north. So it was a
lively bustling place, where news and gossip were
exchanged, along with philosophies and ideas, as well as
trade and commerce.

At first they camped on the outskirts and went in to
exchange some livestock for flour, oil and salt. It was a
good place to break their journey – at least that was the
apparent intention. But Abram and Sarai noticed how,
after a week or two, Terah lost some of his gauntness and
seemed more relaxed. It was evident that he liked this
place.

Things came to a head one night as they were sitting
around the dying fire. They were still living in their tents on
the edge of Haran, and Abram began to suggest that it was
time to move on if they were going to get to Canaan before
winter.

Terah leaned back on his sheepskin-covered couch.

'There is no need to hurry,' he said easily. 'We might as well stay here for the winter.'

Lot was impatient. 'We must move on! The grass will die back soon. We need fodder and space for our flocks and herds!'

Terah refused to be pressured. He waved an arm vaguely in the direction of the sheep pens. 'There will be plenty for everyone, I'm sure!'

Lot persisted. 'I think the townspeople here may not agree with that,' he said firmly.

Abram was watching his father. He could see that the old man was tired of journeying on, day after day. He had left behind the place of sad sweet memories, and while they would never be entirely forgotten, here they did not torment him so sharply and frequently as they had in Ur, with its continual daily reminders and associations. He guessed that if they stopped here now for a season, Terah would never move on.

And so it proved to be. The edge of Terah's appetite to seek something new had dulled. They all agreed to stay on for the winter, but when spring came, there seemed to be no reason to hurry on, and spring turned soon into a scorching summer, when it seemed madness to leave this pleasant plain watered by the river and venture into inhospitable territory, where they could not be sure of finding adequate grazing or water. By the next winter Terah had definitely become more frail, so Haran became their resting place for a number of years.

Sarai still missed Ur, but was glad that they had ceased wandering and had settled down. She liked city life. Although not Ur, Haran was at least a city. It was not so cultured and sophisticated, the buildings were rougher and in her opinion the art and music they found there were definitely on the primitive side. But it did at least have fixed buildings that were eloquent of permanence – and they provided shelter when it rained! Some of those buildings were temples for the worship of the moon god and other deities – another similarity with Ur. It also had bakers' shops, and oil and wine merchants, and other people to talk to besides shepherds. Shepherds had no conversation!

Life here might not be so bad. She could make new friends, and at least it would be easier here to find the distraction she needed. For there was a deep sadness inside her, an emptiness, a sense of failure and shame that she carried constantly. She dreaded loneliness or monotony, because then she had no diversion to help her ignore the cause of her pain. Life in Haran was quite agreeable and not dissimilar in some ways to Ur.

But she was aware that Abram was strangely sad and disappointed. He had set out for Canaan with such high expectations. When they had reached Haran he knew that he must honour his aging father, but he had not anticipated that it would mean staying there for an extended period. Sarai tried to ask him why he felt so troubled.

He struggled to reply. 'There must be something more!' he said at last.

Sarai was mystified.

'Well, let's go back to Ur!' she answered eagerly. 'Ur certainly has more than Haran.'

Abram turned to look at his beautiful wife. He knew it had been hard for her to leave her friends and family and the fun and vitality of Ur. She had not complained, but he knew she was sad. There was another reason for her sadness, he knew well. It was also a source of grief to him, but he would not enter into that right now. He reached out and stroked her cheek. Would she understand if he told her what was in his heart?

'There is an ache in my heart,' he began.

She thought she knew where he was heading, and the great tormenting longing and grief that she tried to keep buried threatened to rise up and engulf her. She turned her eyes away.

'And in mine,' she said in a small low voice.

'Sarai.' His voice was gentle, but he would not be deflected. 'Sarai, I was referring to another pain.' He struggled to open his heart to her. 'There is something in me that is not satisfied. We didn't just leave Ur; we were *called* out. When we all set out for Canaan, I don't know what I expected, but I felt so sure it was right to go! And as we went on, that sense became stronger and stronger. There is a place that calls me; I dream of it at night. I feel it in here.' He placed his hands on his chest. He looked at her again. 'No, not like Ur . . . yet a city, but not made by men.' He stopped and sighed.

It was impossible to explain this inner urge – voice? – that was tugging him, drawing him away from a city that was merely human, and it left his spirit restless, yearning for something, a focus, a companionship that he could not find in Ur or Haran, or even here in his tent with his wife. And now he was in a quandary, worse off than before, for that voice had awakened something in him and he would no longer be content. He had left Ur with all its seeming benefits, but now they had stopped here in Haran, and this was neither one thing nor the other! This was not Ur, but neither was it Canaan! He could not go back, but he felt prevented from going forward. They were stuck, and his heart was still empty.

Sarai sat motionless on the carpet at his feet. Her heart too was aching and empty. Inside her was a vast empty space waiting to be filled. 'What greater pain can there be,' she said dully, 'than to long for a baby who never comes?'

So they settled in Haran, and Abram stifled those compelling urges to move on to something else. He provided for his household and cared for his father, and life went on much the same as it had in Ur.

And then Terah died.

3

The Call

We do not know precisely why Terah decided to move with his family from Ur and set out for Canaan. He did not arrive, but the Bible is very precise that that was his intended destination. He had a definite goal in mind, but he settled for something else along the way.

How often does that happen in a spiritual sense? Jesus told the story of the sower who sowed good seed in different sorts of soil. There was nothing wrong with the seed, but it did not all come to maturity. Some started well but got choked out with weeds. These weeds are interpreted as 'the cares of this life'. They are not necessarily evil or sinful things, but daily pressures and distractions that crowd out the vision that was once so strong.

Ur is thought to have been the early site of the city of Babylon. Running through the Bible from Genesis onwards, Babylon became synonymous with proud human achievement, arrogantly opposed to and independent of God. It epitomises all that sets itself up against the knowledge of God: a separate and opposing kingdom. So it is significant that Terah, Lot and Abraham turned their backs on it and chose Canaan, which was to become synonymous with God's people and God's presence.

Perhaps both Terah and Abraham started out with the same enthusiasm and eager longings for a new start, but Terah got sidetracked. The biblical record is stark in its simplicity: 'They set out to go to Canaan, but when they came to Haran they settled there.' Terah was content with second best. The key word here is 'settled'. It has the quality of relaxing, finding home, making a nest, being cosy.

Everyone wants a home, especially a woman. We find peculiar satisfaction in having our own place with its own front door, and placing our own familiar things around inside. We decorate it with the colours and style that say, 'This is mine and this is how I like it.' Moving house is an uncomfortable operation, not only because of all the legal and financial hassle, but because we have to undo things we have arranged, move into unfamiliar territory, and start again, and we feel strange and disoriented until we have made it our own.

There is nothing wrong with making a home and enjoying it – except when you are on a journey! When you are travelling, it is good to make rest stops every now and then, even stay overnight. But you do not stay long enough to make a home there. You are going somewhere and the intention is to arrive.

There are people whom God has called out, to seek first his kingdom, but they never fulfil their destiny because they get distracted. They make a diversion, intending only to have a break, look around a bit, have a rest, but somehow it becomes a permanent full-stop.

The temptation to settle becomes stronger as we get older. We justify it to ourselves by saying that we have worked hard, we don't have the energy we used to have, we deserve to slow down and let younger blood take the strain. Before we realise what is happening we have changed from being pioneers to settlers.

Terah settled, and Abraham nearly did too, but when God called again, the pioneer spirit that was lying dormant was re-awakened. He was already an elderly man, but he had barely begun to fulfil his life's destiny.

The same was true of Sarah. All we know of her so far is that she was a beautiful woman who was unable to bear children, and that she had left Ur with her husband and father-in-law. Perhaps we have speculated overmuch in assuming that she was a rather unwilling and unenthusiastic travelling companion. But given the knowledge of where she had come from and that she was suddenly expected to head out into the unknown without a clear explanation, I think it is not unreasonable to assume that she might have been regretful and maybe quite resentful. She had yet to meet with the God who can transform lives. She may have been relieved to reach Haran and once again have the opportunity to indulge in the joys of homemaking.

But worse was to come! Just when she had grown used to Haran being her home, she had to uproot all over again.

* * *

Abram was walking through the streets of Haran. He and Lot had been bartering with some merchants and successfully sold a few sheep in return for some carpets, oil, flour and various utensils and provisions. Lot had gone off to arrange for their transport to Abram's spacious dwelling, and Abram decided to linger a while in the town. He found a small inn in the market square and sat down in the shade of a tree outside. Wine and bread were brought out to him and while he ate he watched life passing by. Opposite was a temple built in honour of the moon god. The temple was an impressive edifice known as Ehulhul. Worship of the moon god was a cult widely practised in that part of the world, and Abram was familiar with its customs and beliefs. Indeed, his father may even have participated – perhaps another reason for his willingness to stay here in Haran.

He watched as devotees came and went with their offerings and their garlands of flowers, but also with their hopes and fears and pain and requests. But whereas they left their gifts in the temple, they came out still bearing their pain, with their fears unchanged and their requests unanswered. The god Nannar was apparently unhearing, uncaring and unknowable. He was just an ugly lump of stone, detached and distant like the beautiful, cold, shining moon he was supposed to represent.

Abram sighed and rose to his feet with a heavy heart. There must be something more than this! The old yearning that had nearly been completely submerged, surged up again; that sense that someone was calling him to something beyond that which he could presently see and understand. He walked slowly towards his home on the edge of Haran. As he drew near the huddle of houses, tents and sheep-pens representing all his human wealth and connections, the late afternoon sun was flaming low in the sky. He turned his eyes from their black shadowy silhouettes to the majestic expanse above, gloriously gold and crimson.

'Abram!' He blinked and looked around. He could have sworn someone called his name. But he saw no one. He resumed gazing at the sky drenched in gold light. 'Abram!' There it was again, but was it within or without? He hardly knew, but it had got his full attention. He waited, his ears straining, his heart beating, breathless. When it came, each word was crystal clear, dropping with liquid simplicity into his consciousness: 'Leave your country, your people and your father's household and go to the land which I will show you.'

Abram held his breath, his heart pounding. Awe gripped him, and he stood facing into the flaring beauty of the sunset, his whole being still and listening. There was more.

What he had heard already was remarkable, but what followed was not for his ears alone; it would echo down through countless centuries: incredible promises that would bring faith, direction, identity and purpose to millions who would follow. 'I will make you a great nation, and I will bless you, and make your name great, and so you will be a blessing; and I will bless those who bless you and curse those who curse you and in you all the families of the earth will be blessed.'

By now he was face down in the dust. When he finally struggled to his feet and made his way unsteadily to his dwelling it was dark.

Sarai looked up quickly as he entered. The anxious questions as to where he had been died on her lips when she saw his face. Motioning with her hand she sent away the servant girl who was hovering with a skin of water and brought it to her husband herself. Quietly she offered it to him and sat down at his feet. He took a long drink and several deep breaths before he spoke. When he did, it was not what she wanted to hear.

'Sarai, it is time to leave here.' He spoke with a quiet finality that would not be argued with. 'We are to leave Haran.' At last his eyes lost their faraway look and focused on her. He answered her unspoken question. 'One has spoken to me. I believe it is he whom our forefathers called Elohim Adonai, the Lord God. He called me before to go to a land that he will show me. Now he has spoken again, only this time it is much clearer.'

Sarai's heart was in turmoil. They had left home before! They had wandered about and thankfully had found another home. But now they were to leave again with that same sense of uncertainty. Once more they would have to uproot and abandon the community that had grown up around them over the years and all that she valued in a settled existence. Protests hovered on her tongue, but before they could spill over, Abram spoke again: 'God spoke to me, Sarai, not only about leaving, but about bringing me into great blessing. In fact . . .' here he paused and reached out to her and held her very tightly, as if he was only just beginning to realise the implications of what he was about to tell her. 'He said, "I will make you a great nation and I will bless you and make your name great . . ."' She stood very still within his embrace, and his voice, wobbly with emotion, seemed to come from a long way off. The last words she heard were: '. . . in your seed all the families of the earth shall be blessed.'

A deep silence fell between them. Then, 'Does that mean . . .' She took a deep breath and started again. 'Surely it must mean that we shall have a child?' She stood back from Abram and looked up at him. 'Can we believe him? How can we know? Who is he?'

Abram drew her down onto a couch, and still holding her hand spoke slowly and deliberately: 'I believe he is the same God who spoke to our forefather Noah and commanded him to construct that great boat in which he preserved the lives of hundreds of species of animals when the great flood came. I believe that it was he who confused the language of the people when they attempted to build that massive tower reaching to heaven.' Silence hung heavy in the room. Then he added, 'I believe that Elohim Adonai is the creator God. We can trust him.'

Sarai stood up and wandered around the room, picking things up and putting them down, folding clothes, smoothing cushions. But her mind was busy. Abram watched her and waited. He had some personal knowledge of Elohim Adonai and was coming to trust him, but Sarai had not yet had this advantage. She could only relate to him through her husband. In those days a wife simply went wherever her husband went; there was no independence. Nevertheless, she was a person with feelings! What was she feeling now? He hoped that she would come to a willing decision; he did not want to drag along an unwilling, complaining wife! She was essential to the fulfilment of the word spoken to him. If there were to be a father of a new nation, there must also be a mother! How much better if they were in this together, not just physically, but emotionally and relationally.

Sarai took a few days to think about it. She knew that in the end they would go wherever Abram decided, but somehow this was different from the time when they had left Ur. Then she could see no particular advantage in leaving, but this time the message Abram had apparently received was expanded to include some exciting promises that had big implications for her too. The idea of going to 'a land' was somewhat vague and undefined, but what did they have to lose? Leaving Ur had loosened her previous conviction that she could never be happy anywhere else. Furthermore, here in Haran she was just as barren as she had been in Ur, but it seemed that Abram had received an expectation that if he obeyed Elohim Adonai, he would become a great nation. This was exciting!

Sarai closed her eyes and tried to sort out her thoughts. 'I don't want to go out into the unknown, to wander about seeking something so undefined. How shall we know when we attain it? But I do believe my husband has had an experience that convinces him that this is a genuine call from a genuine God. Here and in Ur I have been a barren woman. If there is a chance that I will become fruitful by taking this path, I will go with him.'

She opened her eyes and smiled at her husband. It was a rather small, scared smile, but her voice was firm as she said, 'I believe you. I will go with you.'

*   *   *

How difficult it is when one partner feels the tug of God in his or her spirit and the other one does not! It can happen that a wife is happily married to a man who is a teacher, a doctor, a salesman or a milkman, then one day he comes home and announces that he is called to be a pastor, an evangelist or a full-time elder. Suddenly her ordered life is turned upside down. This may have huge implications: finances may be drastically reduced; they may have to relocate to a different house or even a different town; children may have to go to a new school and find new friends. And last but not least, what about her own identity? She used to be Mrs Teacher/ Builder/Social Worker or whatever. Now she is to be Mrs Elder. Does this involve a change of image or role?

A friend of mine relates how she was the daughter of a godly pastor, but the pressures on his life caused her to declare that she herself would never marry a pastor. She married a policeman and was happy and content, until one day her contentment was rudely shattered when he came home in a state of high excitement and told her that God had called him into the ministry! He is now a widely respected preacher with a powerful ministry, but there was a time of painful adjustment. Perhaps one of the most difficult aspects was the awareness that God had spoken to the husband and not to her.

It appears from the text in Genesis that God spoke directly to Abraham, and Sarah had little choice but to go along. In those days, women were not expected to resist decisions made by their husbands. Fortunately we live in a day when marriage is seen, rightly, as a partnership between equals; the Lord has promised that all shall hear his voice, male and female. Usually a godly wife will have foreseen a change in direction and be involved with her husband in making the decision. But some women feel perturbed and left behind when their husbands decide to change the course of their lives in response to a call from God.

By the way, a call from God does not necessarily mean

serving him on the staff of a church! We must not make a false distinction between sacred and secular. The Bible doesn't. God wants his servants scattered like salt, permeating society. A call from God may mean a change of location, a change of job or a change of business partner or firm. It does not have to be into what we have come to call 'full-time ministry'.

But whatever calling her husband has received I suggest that for the wife to remain passive is to invite frustration and discontent. We are never to see ourselves as mindless appendages. God wants our wholehearted response to him. But how can we arrive at that if we feel that we are swept up in circumstances we cannot control? Do we just throw up our hands and give in to *fait accompli*? Some wives do give that impression; they just grit their teeth in resignation and plod along behind. Outwardly they may seem to be at one with their husband, but inwardly they feel abused, taken advantage of, and frustrated. They fear that their potential will never be fulfilled because they were trapped into a life that was not their choice.

In Abraham and Sarah's day, marriage was probably not seen as a partnership of equals. Wives were expected to follow their husbands unquestioningly. But we have been called into partnership, and should never feel pushed into something we have no faith for. We do, however, need to be open to the possibility of having our hearts changed, and receiving faith for a new venture. A loving and responsible spouse would only be able to proceed if he and his wife were of one heart in the matter. Both must seek God honestly.

Only recently a young wife recounted to me the struggle she had gone through when her husband knew he must quit his business occupation and give himself to pastoring the church they had been planting. He had been extremely successful in the world of finance – so successful in fact that he was about to be offered a partnership in a prestigious firm, which was quite an honour for a young man. But there came a growing realisation that he was going to have to make a choice: he wanted to do both, but both occupations were increasingly demanding and he was going to have to give up one of them. He knew which one it was going to be.

The wife told me how nervous she was of taking the risk of putting all their energies into building the church and forsaking the security of the large income they were presently enjoying. Her husband waited. Then one day she phoned him at work and told him that God had spoken to her: she did not want to hold him back from obeying the Lord. When eventually he gave in his notice (to an incredulous boss!) it was with the knowledge that his wife was 100 per cent behind him in it. It seemed – it *was* – a sacrifice at the time, but looking at their radiant faces as they told me the story, I felt sure that they were destined to be winners in God's economy!

God wants us to love him with all our heart, soul, strength and mind. This is not a literary device to display a neat poetic symmetry. 'Heart' means that we put him first in our affections; emotion is involved. Loving God is not supposed to be purely a matter of cold will or logic. It is to be the wholehearted, extravagant response of a lover. But it is not only to be all feeling and no sense! 'Soul' indicates the more earthly realm of preferences, choices and personality. God has regard for us as individuals with our own tastes and likes and dislikes. These are not to be indulged rebelliously as a means of stubbornly maintaining our independence, but to be laid at his feet so that he can pick them up and use them to display his own varied character. 'Strength' surely means that we put energies and enthusiasm into following him; a robust loyalty rather than a cool detachment!

But what of the 'mind'? We are to be of sober judgement, of sound mind. God wants us to think things through, and make choices and decisions based on the principles he has revealed. Paul the apostle speaks of 'having the mind of Christ' in 1 Corinthians 2:16 and of his desire to 'present everyone perfect in Christ' in Colossians 1:28. His longing was that the people in his churches would not have to be spoon-fed in terms of being told what to do, but to be able to come to clear convictions because their minds were trained by truth.

So how does this work when a woman is confronted with a twist of events that she has not chosen – one that contradicts her hopes and plans, and seems to be death to her dreams? It may not be a husband's call; it may be an unexpected pregnancy, a long-term illness, the care of an elderly relative, redundancy of employment, the refusal of a visa, even an unexpected invitation to work with orphans or drug addicts. Does she have the right to protest? To object that 'it isn't fair'? To put forward an alternative?

She will probably do all those things initially, but she needs to ask herself some basic questions, beginning with, 'Is God for me or against me?' If she is not armed with objective truth, she will come up with the wrong answer. If her only criteria are her emotions, she will 'feel' that God is against her.

Another question could be, 'What is my goal at this point in my life?' Most of us, if we are honest, will answer something like, 'To make myself feel better' – a not unreasonable ambition! But it is not a long-term solution. We really need to go back to basic principles. A Christian needs to remind herself all her life that she has been bought with a price, and her life is no longer her own. Dying is the only way forward. This applies to men too of course.

How did I come to be where I am? At some point Jesus Christ came to me, loved me, forgave me, saved me and enslaved me. My life is now at his disposal for the purpose of bringing glory to him. This does not mean that I now lie down and take no responsibility for my life. I do not abdicate – I simply judge by different criteria.

To go back to the woman who feels sidelined by a husband's call: she may feel baffled and perplexed that God apparently did not choose to communicate the change of plan to her at the same time as her husband. This was my experience some years ago. My husband had been visiting a church in America that was going through a crisis. We prayed for this church a lot together; in fact we went on an extended fast. As time went by, Terry began to get the impression that God wanted us to go and live in the USA for a while. I had absolutely no feelings about it whatsoever, but I prayed along with him that God would speak to us and make it clear. Terry became more and more convinced and said that he thought God was telling him we were to go for two years. I heard nothing. Other people began to give him confirmatory prophecies and words. I kept praying and looking for verses and listening for directive words. Nothing. Meanwhile, Terry was setting things in motion, applying for visas, making plans. I was not hostile to the idea, but I longed to have my own word from God to settle my heart.

About two months before we were due to leave, our dear friend Nigel Ring was sitting with us having lunch. He turned to me and said, 'What do you feel about all this, Wendy?' I began to cry as I confessed that I had not heard from God at all! I supposed it was all right to go, but I had had no concrete confirmation. Gently Nigel asked, 'What do you think God's original call was to you?'

I thought about it carefully. I had met Terry at Bible college, where I was confidently expecting to receive a call to some specific task, preferably overseas. The call never came. But a young man, Terry Virgo, kept hovering persistently in my range of vision. I felt he was confusing the issue so I resisted his overtures. Then one evening in January, when I was supposed to be studying, God suddenly spoke very clearly to me: 'Terry Virgo is my will for your life. He is the one I am calling you to be with.' From that day on I never doubted that God had brought us together for his purposes. So I was able to answer Nigel's question, and peace entered my heart. I was to go wherever God led Terry, and I did not need a separate word.

Is every leader's wife called to be a leader? Probably not. When her husband becomes a pastor or elder, she does not have to turn into a different animal! She is herself: a wife, maybe a mother, a secretary, a teacher, a nurse. But if the choice has to be made between her job and his call, then her job must not stand in the way of what God is calling him to do. Can a leader's wife have her own sphere of fulfilment and influence? Most certainly; but every now and then it is good to reassess the situation, and if what she is doing is hindering his ministry rather than facilitating it, then there will have to be readjustments. God wants us heart and soul together in building his kingdom. That obviously can happen as both partners work in different spheres, but the kingdom is not advanced if conflict arises and they are found to be pulling in different directions.

As we shall see later, Sarah became a woman of faith. It was not enough that her husband was a man of faith. Later on, action had to be taken that demanded her obedience and faith as well. His faith had to become her faith. Faith pleases God and it is the means by which we bear fruit for him. Do we want to be fruitful for God? Of course we do, but the seed has to fall into the ground and die before it can bring forth fruit.

What about the woman who hears God calling her, but whose husband is deaf to him? Here again Sarah is held up to us as an example, in 1 Peter 3. The apostle wisely advocates that the wife keep her words to a minimum and seek to win her husband by her gentle and respectful demeanour. Her call to follow Jesus does not contradict the principle that she is to continue to regard her husband as the leader in the marriage relationship and to honour him as such, so that he is not belittled or undermined. He goes on to say that she must seek to do this 'without giving way to fear'. If we are in fear, we cannot be in faith, and if we are not in faith, it is easy to resort to manipulation, nagging and preaching at him to get our way. We want to help God along a bit by making our husband see that we have heard from God and he hasn't! Keep quiet and pray for his ears to be opened.

Sarah did not have a perfect marriage. There were times when, seen from our vantage point, she could have been forgiven for abandoning the journey, the call and the husband! But eventually, after much testing, she came to a place not only of faith but of fruitfulness, as we shall see.

4

What Is a Call?

'Having a call' was a familiar phrase in my family's vocabulary, as both my parents were missionary minded. My father's sister was the matron of a missionary hospital in Thailand, and several of my mother's relations were 'on the mission field'. Missionary prayer meetings were held regularly in our home and I was often in meetings where missionaries were showing slides of their work, or a preacher was passionately pleading for people to surrender their lives and offer to serve in missions overseas.

So I grew up with the idea that a call was tied up with serving God in a foreign nation; that it was a definite experience, very individual, very personal and usually came in a meeting, though not always. In spite of reading many excellent missionary biographies, my understanding of missionary life was vague to say the least and was coloured with a tinge of romance and adventure. It was definitely more exciting and more spiritual to serve God in any other nation than one's own! Somehow, crossing the sea turned one into a devout and serious Christian, and the call was a necessary prerequisite – as tangible as if it had dropped out of the sky in gothic lettering on a gilt-edged scroll.

I remember a succession of earnest females coming to stay

with us for weekends, when they would be assessed by a missionary committee, of which my mother was a member. Most of them appeared to have not the remotest awareness of what was current in fashion, they wore no make-up and their conversation was dull. However, to be fair, as I grew up I began to perceive that their lack of attractive clothing owed more to lack of finance than to desire, and some of them were definitely fun to have around. But the thought of joining their ranks and becoming one of them was not inviting, and I remember feeling slightly affronted when one well-meaning missionary lady asked me if I had a 'call'. Perhaps I was thinking of following in the footsteps of my beloved aunt? Now although I loved my aunt dearly, and admired her too, I was not sure about the 'challenge' (another much used word) of responding to the need or following in her footsteps (she was in leprosy work). Intrigued by the idea of going abroad, however, I began to be more open to the possibility of a 'call'.

As a restless and energetic teenager, I began to see increasingly the need for Christian role models who could relate to young men and women, who were outgoing, aware of current trends in clothes and music, who were sharp intellectually and yet confident in their Christian beliefs. I thought sadly of my religious education teacher at school who all too obviously did not believe in the Bible she was required to teach. What a wasted opportunity! All those girls sitting in front of her with the Bible open and yet totally turned off from Christianity as she taught them that it was a load of speculative myths! Many a lesson ended up in fierce debate as I strove passionately to pierce her cool detachment.

So I went to Bible college, determined to get a qualification that would open the door for me to enter the teaching profession. At the same time, through my college years, I kept my heart open to the possibility of a call. I did not view my desire to be a teacher as a call, but somehow I reasoned that I would need a call to be a teacher in another country!

The call did not come. However much I tried to convince myself of an interest in other countries and of the need for workers, and however often I told God that I was ready, willing and eager, I could not kid myself: he was not calling me. But as I have already mentioned, hovering in the wings was a patient young man who seemed to have an interest in me. I knew that a casual relationship was out of the question, but I did not dare embark on one that could lead to marriage and thus divert me from the possibility of a call.

Eventually God spoke very clearly to me those words: 'Terry Virgo is my call on your life.' I was very happy to adapt, but it took me a long time to understand that a call is more than going to a geographical location; it is not only about having a 'feeling' for certain races or nations; it is to do with *being* as well as obeying; it is both general and specific.

So what is it? Is the idea of a call biblical? Should every Christian expect to have one? Or is it only for a select few who are drawn into a specialised ministry? What do we mean by a call?

So often our perceptions are drawn from our backgrounds and get built into our thinking without being checked or challenged. Meanwhile the world goes on, ideologies evolve, develop, change, crumble, and we wake up 20 or 30 years later to find ourselves in a time warp. Church is no longer what it used to be, and especially it is no longer filled with people who think the way we were brought up to think. Thankfully, many ideas we once thought absolutely integral to Christian living have been questioned and found to be grounded merely on what was regarded as the customary norm, not on the word of God at all! For example, behaving quietly and solemnly in church we now recognise as owing more to the English temperament than to the Bible we claim to believe.

A very significant characteristic that was woven into our understanding of Christianity (at least among the evangelicals I was raised with) was the strong individualism that led to Christians making their own decisions and judgements, without much accountability or corporate awareness. Each saw her destiny in terms of her singular fulfilment; each life was a solitary journey undertaken with one's own set of responsibilities, choices, successes and failures. Thus a call was a very personal and private thing – a private response to a private summons.

Ultimately, I am sure that the aim of all Christians was broadly the same: that the gospel would be preached and souls saved. But they largely saw themselves as a bunch of individuals getting on with this task, not as a cohesive force. I think that I believed that the only authentic way to serve God was to preach the gospel. Anything else was second best and therefore there was little recognition of anything other than actual teaching, preaching or talking about God in some way that could be described as Christian work. This put a lot of pressure on people who were not very good at it.

Today there are key words that are very much part of the modern church vocabulary, such as 'body', 'team', 'training', 'gifting', 'moving together', 'corporate vision', 'one people'. Without these, I submit that there is far greater likelihood of competitiveness, success being measured by wrong criteria, anguish about taking the right path, fear of making decisions, misguided motives, and lack of correction. Individualism, I am convinced, often led to a call being something that was qualified by emotion rather than clearsighted, objective judgement.

If we examine how Abraham and Sarah were called we can extract some biblical principles. Abraham is a prime example of a man called by God. The word is used in relation to him many times. First we see him being called out from Ur in Genesis. Then in Isaiah 51:2 we are exhorted to 'look to Abraham, your father, and to Sarah, who gave you birth. When I called him . . .' We are further told by Stephen in Acts 7:2 that Abraham was called to 'leave your country and your people'. Then later on in the New Testament, in Hebrews, we are again directed to consider various heroes of faith, including Abraham and Sarah, who were called out and obeyed. So it would seem that they are prime examples of this genre!

So what can we learn from their call? Can it be a model for us? It certainly must be, as we are told specifically to look to them, particularly in relation to their call (Isaiah 51:2).

In spite of what I have just said about individualism, the call certainly was at first, clearly and specifically, personal. God spoke to a person, to Abraham himself. He had to know in the depths of his being that God was bringing new direction to his life.

And what of Sarah? We are told simply that 'Abram departed, as the Lord had spoken to him . . . He took Sarai his wife . . .'. Abraham's call was her call. She may not have understood this clearly at first, but there came a point at which she had to own it and exercise her own faith, and not just rely on his.

The call involved separation. This couple had to separate themselves from their own family and kinsfolk, and go out to a strange place. They had to depart from family custom, traditions and expectations of the future. This required courage. It also required faith in the one calling them.

So they were called out. But what were they called to? They were called to physically move, it is true, to a geographical location. But the reason they were called was not for self-fulfilment, or to find their destiny. It was to be the start of something much bigger than themselves. In spite of Sarah's barrenness, Abraham was told that he would become the father of a great nation. This nation would become the means of blessing to the whole earth! His call and his obedience to it would initiate a vast plan to start a new nation. So although he was called out as 'one', the intention was that 'many' would come from him. Isaiah is specific about this (Isaiah 51:2). He exhorts his hearers to follow Abraham's example, and then devotes the rest of the chapter to directing our thinking to Zion, Jerusalem, Israel – in short the family that resulted from Abraham's action.

Later Jesus said that those who believe in him are Abraham's children (John 8). We are part of this new family that he started. We are called into it individually when we first believe. We are called out of the darkness of the surrounding world and brought into the light, into the family of God's Son! Wonderful call! And wonderful grace that initiates that call. But from then on our path does not lie along a lonely individual furrow. We are not intended to live solitary lives thinking only of 'my needs', 'my fulfilment', 'my gifting', 'my preferences'. There has to be a change of mindset: this new life is about 'us'. I now have relatives in the body of Christ. In fact I am a part of the body. I have to find my place in it, be integrated, knitted in. So any call I have is in the context of this family. Where the family goes, I go, and where I go, the family goes. We move together, do things together and any plans that we might make are to facilitate the whole.

Probably because of modernism, higher biblical criticism and a renewed emphasis on the social gospel in the first half of the twentieth century, some of the fundamental truths of Christianity got submerged. Doctrines of justification by faith, personal redemption through the cross, the need for conviction of sin and repentance, the power of the blood of Jesus – all preached powerfully by Spurgeon and others at the end of the nineteenth century and by the Salvation Army at the beginning of the twentieth century – had been watered down by mid-century. Then along came Billy Graham and others, preaching a much needed re-emphasis on the need for personal salvation.

The fact that we must be born again must never be diluted or lost. But I for one was raised in evangelical circles that never went beyond this individualism. In fact the word 'church' was so little regarded as to be infrequently used, and then almost with suspicion. I never heard any preaching on the church and the group of Christians that I associated with was called an 'assembly'. 'Church' was reserved for the institutional body that we perceived as cold, unfeeling, official and sorely lacking. We had no theology of the biblical church, and everything was taught from a personal standpoint: my need, my salvation, my Saviour, and therefore my call and my achievements were what mattered. I felt very responsible for my destiny and had no sense of being part of a body.

Naturally there were many Christians whose hearts ached for the lost, but lacking any understanding of the church's commission to work together, many individuals rushed off and formed societies to preach the gospel and to bring education and alleviate suffering in deprived places. It was in this climate that many parts of the Bible originally written to a company of believers were interpreted and preached to individuals. For instance, large parts of Isaiah, prophesied to a backslidden nation, were taken personally.

In the last few decades of the twentieth century, a fresh wind blew and the doctrine of the church came again to the forefront. We began to see that running through the Bible is a theme about a people that God has called out to be his very own treasured possession. Each part of it is brought in by personal dealings with God himself, and each person knows himself to be loved and valued and accepted individually. He will go on hearing God for himself, growing in love for him and maturing in his faith, but part of that maturing is the awareness that we *together* exist for God's glory and to do the work of showing him forth on the earth.

New churches have sprung up and church planting is now seen as a major activity of the people of God. This is because of the deep conviction that only a community can change a community; only a society can alter a society. The church is God's agent for change.

So how does this affect the idea of a call? Is it even a valid concept? Let us go back to our Biblical example of Abraham and Sarah. They were called out of the current world system with its ignorance of the Creator and its idolatrous habits and self-promotion (think of the Tower of Babel). There was a point when they had to make a decision to leave one life behind with its set of values, philosophies, relationships, old habits and customs. This has not changed. In fact it becomes an ever-widening theme in the Old Testament as we see the same thing happening to other individuals, but especially in the history of Israel, a nation called out of slavery in Egypt and brought into the Promised Land. This points forward to Jesus' teaching that we must be born again to enter the kingdom of heaven, and the apostle Paul further elaborates as he writes to the churches about leaving the past behind, reckoning oneself dead to the world and being resurrected into a new life. Each new Christian has to have an individual experience of coming out of an old life and into a new one.

This must be true even for those who have been brought up in a Christian home, as I was. I often thank God for the inestimable privilege and benefits of this, since it meant that I imbibed certain values early on that were good and wholesome. But as I grew into my own individual identity, I had to examine my convictions and determine whether or not they truly *were* convictions, or simply 'moulding'. This is an ongoing process all through one's life, of course. But the Bible speaks of not being conformed to the thinking of this world (Romans 12:1–2) and if one is not alert, it is easy to unthinkingly take on board current philosophies and mind-sets that are not the product of biblically based thinking, but of this 'present evil age', as the apostle Paul put it. Whatever our background, we must realise that we are called out of the easy flow of 'everyone's doing it', or 'I'm not hurting anyone' or tolerance for its own sake. Our ethics must not be situational, but based on the absolutes presented in the Bible, and this constitutes part of our calling: the ongoing and continuous renewal of the mind.

So, yes, each Christian must, by definition, have had a call: called out, but now called into something. And this is where we need to change our thinking from individualism to corporatism. In other words, it is no longer just 'me' but 'us'. Where are *we* going, and what is the part that God has chosen for me to play in the wider scheme of things?

Abraham and Sarah founded a nation. We are part of that nation. Abraham is our father and Sarah our mother. Jesus said so. I am part of a body, not a separate limb. I cannot simply decide that I will go to Zimbabwe or Manchester without reference to what the rest of the body is doing. And yet I am an autonomous being, with likes and dislikes, desires and preferences; with relationships, abilities, gifts; with a body and a personality. Does God no longer regard me as a single entity?

God loves his church and every individual in it. He loves each part and the sum of the parts. He speaks to each member personally, and he speaks to the whole body. The body is his bride and he loves her, and he wants us to love the bride too.

So when we ask, 'What would you have me to do?' he has

many replies, a different one for each member. But the aim is the same: 'How can I, as a member of his body, best serve God?' Or put another way, 'How is the body serving God, and how can I be included in that?'

Each member is called. First of all, the call is to be like him, so we are all called to holiness, love, compassion, faith and kindness – in fact to 'walk as Jesus did' (1 John 2:6). We are also 'called . . . into fellowship with . . . Jesus Christ' (1 Corinthians 1:9). This is the 'high calling' that we are to pursue, which Paul the apostle talks about in Philippians 3:14: the upward call of knowing him and being like him.

So it appears from the New Testament that our call as believers has more to do with receiving from God than it has with doing. This is so far removed from the old concept that I was brought up with. I had thought that in order to be a 'real' Christian, I had to have a call to be a missionary or some kind of full-time worker. Any other sort of Christian was definitely inferior! How releasing to find that instead I am 'called' to be a partaker in blessings that Christ has already secured for me! And not only that, it is in the context of a new family and we are going along together.

Now it may be that, as I am going along in my Christian walk, growing in the gifts and graces that God supplies, I may begin to hear a voice behind me saying, 'This is something I want you to do.' But because I have found security under the authority in the church family, I will submit what I think I am hearing to those over me in God. Together we will seek God, and that authority will either endorse that it is God speaking, so that I am supported and strengthened in this new direction, or it will be perceived that it is not God, and a possible disaster will be averted.

This is of immense value. It means I am no longer wholly self-dependent on direction for my life, but I have the security of others around me, helping me and encouraging me. On the other hand, it also means that the family of God can be enriched by the energy, creativity and resources poured in by many members. If the shepherds of the flock are receiving clear direction from the Lord to plant out a new congregation, say, or to start a shelter for the homeless, or to send out people to a project in Mexico, then there will be people in the body who will feel God is equipping them to be part of what the body is already doing.

In any event, I am glad that I am called to be part of the family of God, partaking in all the excitement of bringing in his kingdom. Life is so much less complicated now that I have stopped trying to find my 'personal call'. Basically, it is doing whatever I find in my hand to do, and to do it with a whole heart. Once I have the foundation in place, which is Christ, I can do any job, any career, marry or not marry, work overseas or at home, ostensibly 'for God' or not. No job is more sacred or spiritual, or carries more points! The aim is to be a means of bringing Jesus' life into whatever I do as a member of his body.

Whatever God wants us to do, he will give us the grace to do it. That is why there is no point in feeling guilty if we are not doing what another is doing. They have grace for it; we don't. There is no point in being competitive either, for the same reason. God gives specific grace for specific tasks. Paul had a specific call to be an apostle, and he was given the grace for it. I have been given the grace to be my husband's wife, with all that that involves!

Are you a secretary? Be a good one. Are you a nurse, a teacher, a shop-worker, a traffic-warden? Are you married or single? A parent, even a grandparent? You are called. Whatever you are, you are called to have fellowship with Jesus, to be like him and to bring glory to him. What a calling!

5

Travelling to Canaan

It had been weeks since they had left Haran, and it lay far behind to the north-east. Compared to the inhospitable landscape before her it now seemed to have been a haven of all things civilised, comfortable and reassuring. Days merged into a blur of sun, sand, stones and endless horizons that wobbled and shimmered in the relentless heat. The sheep straggled along in pathetic little groups, thinner every day. The camels padded silently, strung out along the sand dunes in long thin lines, their passengers comatose. Several carts pulled by pairs of oxen rumbled along carrying utensils and tent poles and furniture.

Most of the time Sarai travelled in one of these. She kept a sharp eye on the water supplies held in leather bottles suspended from camels and heaped in the back of the carts. Whenever they reached an oasis, which wasn't often, her first thought, after a drink of fresh water, was to refill the bottles. The difficulty was to keep to tracks that led from oasis to oasis. They dare not be far from water for more than a couple or at most three days. They could carry water for their own needs, but to supply for all their livestock as well was impossible. The camels had an amazing capacity and could carry enough resources in their own bodies to keep going for days, even weeks, but the same could not be said for the sheep and goats and human beings.

Abram sent scouts ahead to find pasture and water and to gather news along the trail from any other travellers. Each night they would make a rough camp, putting up some of the tents and cooking simple meals over a fire. Then they would jog on again the next day. When they came to a well or oasis, they settled there for a few days, to recover their strength, wash clothes and regroup their resources for the next stretch of the journey. So they ambled on, day after day.

They kept going in a southerly direction. The terrain was hard, and the days monotonous, but Sarai thought that her husband, now 75, seemed more alive and vigorous than ever. There was a sense of energy flowing from him as he strode among the flocks in the evening, examining the ewes and giving orders to the shepherds. His head was held high and his shoulders back as he swung along, swishing the air with his staff, calling to servants, attending to a limping camel or a pregnant ewe. It was he who decided where and when to stop and make camp, what animal to slaughter for food, how long to stay.

She had plenty of time to think about it and to observe him. She wondered how much his call from the God Elohim Adonai had to do with this increased awareness of authority, and purposefulness. Although the journey seemed rambling and slow, he seemed to have regained a sense of direction and in some way a heightened sense of identity. He really believed that he was going to be a father. What was more, he really believed that he was going to be the ancestor of a vast multitude! There was more activity in their tent at night than there had been in years. Sarai herself hardly dared to hope. She was still a beautiful woman, and she was glad that her husband still found her so desirable. The rigours of travelling through the desert did not seem to have diminished his potency or his appetite, and now he was not backward in his attempts to make the promise of fatherhood become fact.

After some weeks of crossing the harsh and inhospitable desert, there came a noticeable change in the landscape. First, a line of green hills appeared on the horizon, the dusty ground gave way to softer soil, the sparse grass became more lush and verdant. Plants and trees became plentiful and soon they were on a well-watered plain, on which stood a walled city. This turned out to be Damascus, another well-known stopping point for merchants, and a pleasant and inviting place. Here the travellers allowed themselves a period of relaxation. After the necessity of carefully hoarding their water supplies and rationing their food, it was very liberating to be able to drink as much as they wanted, to bathe luxuriously in streams and pools, and to stuff themselves with dates, nectarines and peaches.

This was a pleasant interlude, which resulted in more than enough time to relax and replenish their energies. A good deal of bartering went on among the many merchants coming and going. Abram's and Lot's flocks were quite numerous by now. They sold some of their stock and brought fresh blood into their flocks, and Abram began to look for another more experienced shepherd. One day in the market-place he came upon a young man named Eliezer, who impressed him with his eager eyes and bright smile. During their time in Damascus he got to know him quite well and found him to be intelligent and knowledgeable. He had an easy personality, but was always respectful. When eventually Abram and Lot moved on, Eliezer went with them and became Abram's personal steward.

They continued to travel south. Rolling green hills stretched before them and the plains were well watered and fertile. They were now on the edge of Canaan. Sarai looked around her eagerly. This was the place that Abram had dreamed about, the land for which he had forsaken the great city of Ur, the country that in his heart he knew he would ultimately possess! Would these hills and plains one day be filled with the dwellings of families that all derived their existence from them?

Their route lay over the Golan Heights, which was hard going with all their entourage, but the views were breathtaking and the green and blue of the surrounding hills, fading into purple in the distance, soothed her spirit after the arid barren wilderness before Damascus.

One day they crested a ridge and there before them lay a beautiful stretch of water, pear-shaped and glistening among the quiet hills. Slowly they circled round it and found a pleasant place above the shore to pitch their tents. That night their usual menu of lamb in some form or other received the welcome addition of fish caught from the lake. They ate with relish and the conversation around the fires that night was more than usually animated and light-hearted.

As the embers died down, Sarai leaned back and gazed at the brilliant stars overhead. Abram heard her sigh of contentment and smiled at her, his face caught in the glow of the dying fire. She smiled back, softly, dreamily, reflecting with a mild surprise that she had never been happier than she was right now. Strange, considering that she had left behind things that she had once thought essential to a fulfilling life. Here she was, meandering along day by day to some vague destination, but she was learning to look forward rather than back, and in the meantime she had a loving husband and the promise of a fruitful life ahead.

She pondered on that promise. They had risked everything for the hope that had been set before them – the hope of a son who would be the first of a great nation. Dimly she was coming to perceive that this was not different or separate from the longing that Abram had hidden in his heart before they had ever left Ur. There, he had tried to communicate to her a vision that he had seen of a city, and it was for desire of that city that he had taken his family and gone to find it. Now she was beginning to realise that the vision of a new nation and the vision of the city were but two aspects of the same thing.

Galilee! How evocative is the name of that lake to us! But then it was known as Chinnereth. Imagine her now wandering down to the lakeside. It was dark, but the stars and the moon provided enough light for her to be able to pick her way to the water's edge. The wavelets lapped placidly on the stones and glinted in the moonbeams. All around, the dark silhouettes of the Galilean hills arose. Quiet. It was so quiet. She breathed in slowly, savouring the peace of the place. A little bubble of joy welled up in her. 'This land will be our land,' she whispered to herself.

Did a sudden glimpse flash across her inward eye? Fishing boats on the water, men throwing out nets, reefing sails, straining at oars, calling to one another; lights on the shore of small towns teeming with people, laughing, loving, living; small boys splashing, young girls paddling, women washing, men mending nets; families. Descendants from her and Abram. She opened her eyes. The lake lay before her, serene and empty in the moonlight. Would it be populated by their offspring? Could it really happen?

They moved on, but now as they journeyed it was no longer with the detached interest of the traveller passing through. It was with the sharp-eyed curiosity of prospective new tenants who want to see what the new home is like.

For a while they stayed near a very meandering river that wriggled its way with many curves and bends through bushes and trees. They learned that this was the River Jordan. But eventually they came to higher ground. On a plain between two high hills was a great oak tree, and here they pitched camp. It was an ideal resting place, sheltered between the hills, with plenty of pasture and access to water. Sarai busied herself with disposing of rugs and bedding around the interior of the tent, making it as homelike as possible. She sang happily to herself as she arranged their familiar possessions. Through the tent door she could see the rolling hills surrounding them and the branches of the oak tree waving gently in the evening breeze.

Abram came to the tent door and stood watching her. She turned and faced him, her still lovely face contented and glowing, and he came towards her and took her hands. They went and stood together in the doorway of the tent, and looked out at the peaceful scene. The sun was beginning to sink above the hill behind them, casting a golden glow and long shadows over the valley.

'So, this is Canaan,' he remarked unnecessarily. 'Are you glad we came now?'

She laughed and squeezed his hand. 'I love it!' she admitted. 'This is a beautiful country. I shall be content if we never leave it. O Abram! If only we can raise a family here! I feel as if we have come home.'

'We have the Lord's promise,' replied Abram, encircling her waist with his arm. 'Here we shall be blessed.'

He did not spend long that night making sure all was well with the flocks and shepherds. Eliezer had everything under control, and Abram carried the image of his wife's happy face as he did his nightly round. When he came back, she was waiting for him in the inner chamber of the tent. Her last thought as they came together in the darkness was, 'Surely now I shall conceive!'

She often looked back at that time as one of the happiest

of her life. After all the wanderings and uncertainty, they had found a resting place. But it was not to remain like that for long. Soon another period of testing would assail them and she would be engulfed again with doubt and frustration.

In a fold of the hills on the other side of the valley stood a walled city. This was Shechem, a settlement of Canaanites who not only pastured their flocks of sheep on this fertile plain but had also cultivated the land around them and were producing crops of grain and vegetables. Abram and his servants met them from time to time in the course of daily life. Their presence vaguely disturbed him. They were not particularly hostile, but they regarded Abram and his party with cautious reserve.

Abram was disquieted by their ownership, by the sense that they were in possession of the land. How did this affect the word that the Lord had spoken to him? Had he indeed meant that Abram and his descendants would be the inheritors? These Canaanites seemed very secure in their dwellings, very established, and not at all likely to tamely relinquish their hold on the land. What, if anything, was he to do about God's promise? Should he make some sort of challenge? But on what grounds? He had no desire for outright confrontation, and certainly didn't have sufficient resources to carry on a war.

But the Lord had called him here! He had left everything else behind in the understanding that God would guide him to Canaan and that he and his descendants would possess it. Should he not further demonstrate his faith by claiming ownership? Day by day he pondered his position. Sarai watched him, troubled by his inner turmoil. What was he supposed to *do* with this word?

She herself had been buoyed up by the very fact that they had arrived at their destination and was enjoying the sense of being settled. She was sad that he was not sharing her peace. Then one morning she awoke and found that he was not by her side. Sleepily she groped her way to the doorway and looked out. It was dawn: quiet, soft and dew-laden. Coming towards her on the wet grass was her husband. Hastily throwing a shawl around her shoulders, she went out to him.

'What are you doing?' she asked.

'I am going to look for some large stones,' was the unexpected reply. He grinned at her astonished face, then answered her unspoken question. 'I am going to build an altar in this place to the Lord God.' His voice was strong and vigorous, and in the growing light she could see a joy in his face that had been missing for a while.

She tugged his hand. 'Tell me what has happened!' she begged.

'In the night,' he said quietly, 'I could not sleep. I left the tent and walked among the hills. The Lord God appeared to me. He said, "To your offspring I will give this land."'

Sarai could feel his hand trembling, and awe fell upon her too.

He looked her full in the face. 'He will, Sarai, he will. He will do it in his time. I don't know how or when, but I believe him. I have his word and I have to wait for him. That is all I can do.'

Around them the world was turning pink with the rising sun's rays. They stood together, this childless elderly couple in a foreign land, and believed God that one day this land would be populated with their offspring. It was ludicrous, outrageous. But unknown to them, heaven was applauding.

Abram called Eliezer and they organised men to find large rocks. They dragged them to a flat place near the majestic oak tree and there Abram built an altar to God. Now they had before them every day, when they awoke and all day long, a tangible expression of their faith in a God who had spoken personally, and a reminder of his promise.

* * *

Centuries later, the writer of the epistle to the Hebrews was pondering the examples of many heroes who lived by faith. 'Without faith it is impossible to please God,' he stated robustly (Hebrews 11:6), and went on to demonstrate that faith was the governing factor in lives full of purpose and achievement. They embraced a pilgrim existence; they made choices that caused them to eliminate things that were not wrong in themselves, but would have hindered them from reaching their goals.

Faith was expressed in strange ways for some of them. For example, of all the things that could have been written about Joseph, what is picked out is that he 'gave instructions about his bones' (Hebrews 11:22)! The point is that although he did not personally witness the fulfilment of the promises concerning the inheritance of Canaan by the Israelites, he was still in faith that it would happen even after his death, and he wanted his bones to be a silent part of it.

Abraham's altar is a similar declaration: a pointing forward in belief, a monument to the veracity of God's word. But an altar speaks of other things too. It is like a milestone; a marker that says, 'Here God spoke, and I had to lay down my questions and hesitations. I had to put something to death in order to move forward.' Altars speak of dying, of sacrifice. There is a process of relinquishment, of leaving, of reckoning something to be dead; so loss is involved.

But it is also an offering, a desire to devote, to give, to embrace, and here for the Christian is the positive side of sacrifice. It is because we have seen something better that we are willing to leave old things behind. Whatever it is that we are putting to death, we are doing it while looking up into the face of one who has spoken and captured us, and everything else fades into insignificance.

Sometimes faith is expressed by waiting. Not only is faith necessary, but patience as well. 'Through faith and patience [we] inherit what has been promised' (Hebrews 6:12). We cannot make God's promises happen. We have to wait for his time and then act. Sometimes his promises are for a succeeding generation; sometimes they are for next week! The writer to the Hebrews encourages his readers to be diligent, so patience is not a passive thing. It means getting on with life, doing what you have to do, but in the expectation that at some point God is going to turn up and do what he said he would do. He is not a predictable, push-button God who works by formulae.

Many years were going to elapse before Abraham and Sarah would see the beginning of the promises coming to pass, but they are there in the New Testament as heroes of faith: those who kept going and, against all odds, believed God.

6

The Desert

After a time, they moved on. Although Sarai felt that this land was her home, they were nomads now; they had flocks and herds and were always looking for fresh pasture. Abram wanted to be acquainted with Canaan, so they journeyed on to Bethel, further south, in the hill country but well watered. Here Abram built another altar, affirming his faith in the Lord.

Sarai was sad when Abram announced that it was time to be on the move again, but the rains had not come. The green land was turning yellow and brown. Streams were drying up, rivers were low and getting lower. They must seek out water and pasture. The dread spectre of famine was threatening the land!

It was several years now since they had left Haran, and she had enjoyed this peaceful interlude in her life. The baby she longed for had not yet appeared, but she was still hopeful and she loved this land. But now Abram proposed going further south, and they began to trek down the ever-descending route that led to a steely grey stretch of water. The air was humid and still. They did not stop at the first town they passed, or the second; Sodom and Gomorrah they were called. The water lay turgid and unrippling before

them, and the heat grew ever more oppressive. They straggled on slowly through the thick air beside this inland sea.
Its waters were sour but usable. Some years later, there
would be a catastrophic event that would make them for
ever poisonous, full of caustic chemicals, deceptive but
deadly to all forms of life, but for now they were still sustaining to life.

Eventually they came to the southern end of the Salt Sea.
Before them stretched an arid, unwelcoming landscape.
Surely they would now turn round and retrace their steps to
the pleasant hills around Shechem! Sarai waited anxiously
for Abram to issue instructions. She had felt suffocated in
this still, solemn valley, so humid and stagnant. She could
not breathe here. She longed for the soft breezes and the
soothing greens and blues and browns of the fertile plains.
Here the light bounced off the sand and rocks, making her
head and eyes ache. Her face was screwed up into a perpet-
ual frown as she narrowed her eyes against the dazzling sun,
and she could feel her skin tightening, drying, aging. It was
not a happy thought – especially as she knew that other parts
of her body were also no longer functioning with efficiency.

On they went down into the Negev, the harsh unforgiving
desert region between Canaan and Egypt. The soft air of the
Canaan hills was now a distant, wistful dream. Abram was
anxious for his household and flocks. Sarai was depressed.
The carefree buoyant mood she had enjoyed back in
Shechem and Bethel had receded into an erratic mix of
emotions, of which despondency was the uppermost.
Sometimes, in the stifling heat of her tent in the slumberous
afternoon when all the rest of the company were dozing, she
felt downright panic-stricken. What was going to happen to
them? They were drifting further and further away from the
land of promise! They would get lost in the wilderness and
never get out! And with these fears her old grief came

rushing back. She still had not conceived – she would never conceive! She, with her dried-up womb, would become a dried-up corpse in the desert.

As she had feared, Abram gave orders to continue moving in a southerly direction. Anxiously she faced him. 'Can we not go back?' she pleaded. 'This land is barren! What is the point of going this way? Everyone we meet who comes up from Egypt tells us of the horrors of the desert. There are too many of us to find water and pasture for the flocks . . .' She wrung her hands and looked at him pleadingly.

Abram was stubborn. 'Do you think I don't know all that?' he demanded roughly. 'But we have come too far in this direction to turn back now, at least for a while! The rains have failed back in Canaan, so the harvest is poor there too. Our best hope is to keep pressing on to Egypt. They are not so dependent on the rains there. I have heard that their great river, the Nile, floods every year, keeping the land watered. Spring rains come down from regions up river, swelling its volume and spreading over a great area so that grain grows abundantly. We must make our way there!'

She clung to his hand and sobbed. But the more she protested, the more adamant he became. He had set his course and he would not turn back. But he did not build an altar here; perhaps there was no sense that this was God's direction for them.

Sarai could not shake free of her feeling of foreboding, and the sense of being in exile from the land that God had promised them. They were driven from it by famine – something they had known little of before. In Ur they had lived in plenty; in Haran they had prospered; in Canaan they had settled in a green and pleasant land, believing it to be their inheritance; so what had gone wrong that they now found themselves hungry and wandering in this harsh and alien place?

The sense of dread that they were going in the wrong direction increased and oppressed her. Everything in her wanted to turn around and run in the opposite direction, but day after inexorable day, they pushed on south-west in the hot, harsh desert. The sheep straggled along, seeking what pasture they could in the dry scorched earth. Every evening, when Abram went around his flocks, he found they had dwindled, as some had fallen down and died in their tracks: they would leave a pathetic trail of bleached bones behind them. Always, a few vultures circled lazily high above, waiting ominously.

Sarai felt desperate, afraid, suffocated with terror that one of those menacing shadows would one day swoop down and tear at her parched emaciated body. She would be left alone here to rot and provide food for scavengers. Inheritance? Destiny? Promise? She could have laughed in derision, but it would have come out as a scream. Confusion had replaced direction, and a profound sense of loss now replaced the former bliss of feeling she had come home.

The only respite was the occasional rest at a well or small oasis, islands in the midst of a sea of drought. In her fear she withdrew from Abram and turned in on herself. She could not articulate her emotions. She felt cut off, not only from her former home and country – that had ceased to be a problem to her long ago – but from the secure feelings she had come to enjoy: the security of knowing they were going somewhere with purpose; that they had direction and expectations. Those good feelings had kept her strong and happy. They had helped to prosper their marriage relationship as they had shared the discoveries of the new land. They had laughed and loved and looked forward eagerly to the future.

Now each day was a blur of misery, trudging through the desert towards Egypt, further and further away from the land of inheritance. Water now became the thing of supreme importance; everything else dwindled into insignificance. Her goal now was simply to survive.

*   *   *

Deserts are a normal feature of walking with God. Jacob, Joseph, Moses, David, Elijah . . . all had their desert experiences. The apostle Paul spent years in the desert, and even Jesus went through six gruelling weeks of hunger, thirst and temptation in the Judean wilderness. The trouble is, we read of these great people learning through intense times of testing, nod wisely and turn the page, but somehow it comes as a huge shock to us when we too encounter our deserts!

Why does the Christian pathway have to go through such territory? I asked myself that question over and over again a few years ago. One morning I was listlessly pushing a broom around the kitchen floor, tears trickling down my face. It seemed that for months I had felt limp and dreary in a grey world. The landscape ahead looked flat and featureless, and when I looked back it appeared much the same. The days of joy and vibrant energy, of hopes, dreams and expectations, belonged to another country, dimly remembered, like a line of distant hills, a past horizon.

Suddenly a phrase came to mind: 'The Valley of Baca'. It kept thrusting itself insistently into my consciousness. I repeated it to myself and dredged up some more from my memory. The Valley of Baca was a place of weeping. It didn't sound too promising, but it did describe where I was! I went and found my Bible. There it was, in Psalm 84:6–7.

> Blessed are those whose strength is in you,
> who have set their hearts on pilgrimage.
> As they pass through the Valley of Baca,
> they make it a place of springs;

the autumn rains also cover it with pools.
They go from strength to strength,
till each appears before God in Zion.

So much here spoke directly to me of my situation. First, it is addressing those whose hearts are in the right place. Like Abraham and Sarah, they have left all to follow God. Pilgrimage is in their hearts; not self-seeking, or worldly ambition, or carnal appetites. They are people who have known the blessing and strength of God. This was encouraging. I had not fallen into sin or lost my way. It was part of the natural course of pilgrimage; it cannot be avoided, and there is no short cut. You just have to keep going.

But this was the next encouragement: 'they pass through'. Blessed words! You don't stay there for ever. You don't camp out indefinitely. There will be an end to this. It is not a cul-de-sac. To the uninitiated, deserts are confusing. Tracks are faint or undiscernible. After a while the fear sets in that you have lost your way entirely and are going round and round fruitlessly in circles. You are wasting energy going nowhere. A terrible panic assails you that you will just go on and on, never progressing, never getting out, doomed to roam about until you drop in exhaustion and despair, crushed, abandoned, finished. You will never attain anything because you are destined to become one more pathetic heap of bones dried out in the sun, another silent testimony to another failure. So the idea of 'passing through' is like a signal of hope. You won't die in the desert; you will get through and live.

The Valley of Baca is the place of weeping. It is the place of facing up to our weakness; of not being able to hide it any longer; of realising that we are no better or stronger than the next Christian traveller. The desert reduces us all to the basics. Here, no gifting or intelligence or money or education is going to make the least bit of difference. There is only one thing worth having in the desert: water!

Without water we are dead. We must have it; it is imperative to sustain life. Nothing else matters. But we have to dig for it. We don't know when the rain will come, so we cannot sit around and wait for it. We must find water where we can. So dig. Go to where you know the water is likely to be. You don't feel like reading the Bible? Neither did I. You don't feel like going to meetings? Me neither. But it's a choice: find water or die. Make the effort to go to where there is likely to be some. You might only find a cupful, and you might despise it, saying to yourself, 'Well, I was hoping for a deluge and look what I got: a meagre cupful! And it's brown and bitter.' What will you do with it? Pour it away? How stupid would you be? It could be the difference between life and death! At least it will keep you going until the next cupful.

So do what you know to do: read the Bible, mix with other believers, go to prayer meetings, sing worship songs. This isn't about whether you feel like it; this is about survival. Get some water down you, fast! Psalm 84:6 says, 'they make it a place of springs'. The responsibility is yours. The desert is what you make it.

But what news awaits in the next verse: 'The autumn rains also cover it with pools.' All of a sudden it's raining. What a transformation! What bliss! No more digging – just sit there and let it rain! Then, as your strength builds up, you can run about in it, and dance and sing and shout for joy, with your face turned up to let it pour all over you. And you didn't do a thing to make it happen. No one can make it rain. But how we need it! God knows that; he makes it rain. He sees us struggling away, clinging on to what we know, and believing his promises against all evidence to the contrary. He sees us faithfully getting on with the job, sometimes growing weary in well doing. Not much is happening. Apart from the occasional oasis, days are monotonous. We keep going because there is not much else we can do.

Then, without warning, the skies darken with black clouds, lightning flickers and something in our spirits lifts and stirs and quickens. He's here again! Big fat drops of rain fall on our parched, dried-out souls, and we let it soak in and plump out the withered, dehydrated cells. We draw in lingering, luxurious breaths of the sweet smell of rain on dry ground. How wonderful it is to rest in the sheer luxury of his presence after such a long absence!

We come up out of the desert wiser and stronger. We have learned what is really important: water. Jesus. Only he can give us what we need for life. He has promised never to leave us or forsake us. He never abandons us completely in the desert, but he wants us to want him, not to take him for granted.

We also learn – sometimes to our astonishment – how very weak we really are, how near to failure, how vulnerable to despair, how quick to believe the worst. When we set out on our pilgrimage, we did so with such high hopes, such joyful anticipation of what we were going to do for God. God loves that – he does not despise our longings and intentions – but sometimes he has to disillusion us about ourselves so that we are desperate for him alone.

The goal of the road of pilgrimage is to see God, and the road runs straight into the desert. Eventually it comes out the other side, but meanwhile the goal has not changed. As the pilgrims come up from the desert, the promise is renewed: 'They go from strength to strength, till each appears before God.' This is a foretaste of what is written in the New Testament: 'We all, with unveiled face, beholding . . . the glory of the Lord, are being transformed . . . from glory to glory' (2 Corinthians 3:18, NKJV).

Those verses in Psalm 84 became a lifeline for me at a

barren time. I believed I would pass through, and I renewed
my faith in God's promises never to leave me. I dug doggedly
for water and always there was enough to take me on to the
next spring. Then one day in a prayer meeting, I had a vision
of the Lord standing before me. The desert, with all its
harshness, its rocks and dust, its corpses of failure lying in
the sand, was behind him. He stretched out his hands to me
and said, 'Who is this coming up from the desert leaning on
her lover?' (Song of Songs 8:5). I was undone.

Soon, the rains came.

7

Egypt

Abram stared uneasily at Sarai as she walked gracefully towards him, one slender arm held up to steady the large water pot on her shoulder. It was unbelievable that she was in her sixties! As she swayed up the hill, her long black hair swinging behind her, and the folds of her skirt parting to show a shapely leg, she could pass for a woman in her thirties.

As they had approached the borders of Egypt, they left the desert behind and began to appreciate the changes in the landscape. Small streams appeared, along with cultivated fields irrigated by the ingenious contraptions rigged up by the Egyptian farmers. At last they were able to buy fresh corn and add some fruit and vegetables to their diet. The scrawny sheep and goats began to flourish again as they grazed in good pasture. The people were cautiously friendly – curious but not hostile. Nevertheless, Abram was wary, particularly as he noticed that his wife appeared to attract attention. After the oppression of the desert, she seemed to blossom in this agreeable climate. No longer swathed from head to foot in voluminous garments to keep off the glaring sun, she brought out some of her pretty robes again, which showed off her comely figure. He appreciated the change.

But he could not help noticing that admiring glances were often thrown in her direction, and many dark Egyptian eyes followed her when she bartered in the market-place or went to the well. He felt nervous in this foreign land. Suppose one of those handsome Egyptians had evil intentions? As her husband, he could end up with a knife in his back. He sighed. A beautiful wife was a delight, but also a potential hazard!

The rigours of the nomadic life had left Sarai no time to settle into middle age. She was not one to sit around in the sun vegetating. She was always energetically involved with whatever needed to be done. She had become an expert at serving up lamb in many delicious dishes; she not only competently and quickly kneaded and shaped bread, she personally helped to grind the corn. Although she had plenty of maidens to supervise and instruct, she was often alongside them as they did the work. Her arms were not flabby but sinewy and strong, her back was straight; and if her complexion, which was less dark than Canaanite or Egyptian skin, had suffered a little from the dry climate, her eyes were bright and alert, and beautiful even teeth were visible when she smiled her lovely smile.

She did so now, as she handed down the water jar to a waiting girl who was filling basins in the cooking area. Her husband continued to watch appreciatively as she flexed her back muscles and called one of the other girls to her. 'Fetch me the flask of almond oil,' she asked. 'Bring it to my tent.'

The girl soon reappeared with the requested item. Quietly, Abram intercepted her and took the flask of oil. 'I will take it to her,' he said. He went in and found his wife removing her outer garment. She looked up, surprised, as he entered. He smiled reassuringly. 'Lie down,' he said. She lay, face down, and he tipped some oil into his palm and gently began to rub it into her shoulders and back with long sweeps of his hand. She relaxed, and remarked, 'Those water pots are heavy. They make my shoulders ache!'

'You should send one of the servants!' he reproved her. 'You must not strain this beautiful back!'

She smiled. 'While I can still do these things I will!' she asserted.

His fingers moved down her arm and he gently massaged her hand, rubbing the fragrant oil into the palm. 'No wonder your skin is still so soft,' he observed. 'Sarai, I am proud of you. You are so beautiful, and you keep yourself young and strong. You look like a young woman!'

She laughed and made a disclaiming gesture, but was obviously pleased. She turned over and sat up. 'I am glad I please you,' she murmured.

Abram replaced the stopper of the little bottle and stood up. 'You don't know how much!' He bent and stroked her face, admiring again the curve of her cheekbone, then cupped her face in his hands and kissed her. 'You don't know how much,' he repeated, and added, 'I hope these Egyptians will keep their distance!'

He went out, leaving her lying on the cushions, relaxed and drowsy. But his last remark had puzzled her, and she pushed it around in her mind, wondering why he had said it. She picked up the bottle of oil again and began to rub it into her feet and ankles, examining them critically. The oil was working into the skin, soothing the inevitable dryness, but her toes were straight, her legs were shapely and she had no varicose veins. Well, there was a reason for that! No babies – no varicose veins! She sighed. It was a small compensation in her view; she would rather have risked the veins!

She turned her attention to her hair, and picking up a tortoiseshell brush, began to brush its shining length with long rhythmic strokes. A few grey hairs were discernible here and there. She pulled some out, then decided that if she twined her hair into an intricate plait they would not show so much.

She put on a clean robe and went outside. The heat of the day had subsided; it was late afternoon. A pleasant view greeted her. After the terrors of the desert, she revelled in the green foliage of trees and vines, of fields thick with green spears of early wheat. Not far away was the river, one of the channels of the great Nile delta. She could see the sails of the dhows plying up and down, and hear the shouts of people fishing and washing and digging in the fertile yellow-brown mud of the waterlogged fields. She flung back her head and breathed in deeply of the rich and varied aromas.

When she opened her eyes, she was suddenly aware of a couple of men standing nearby. They were dressed in the short white robes of the Egyptians, with colourful sashes around their waists and white embroidered head-dresses. They seemed to be men of some standing, for not far off a couple of elegant chariots were waiting with magnificent horses in richly adorned harnesses, held in check by two servants.

Quickly Sarai glanced around and was relieved to see Eliezer advancing. He greeted the men courteously and called servants to bring seats and wine. Soon they were settled under a shady tree. Sarai waited until she could see Abram approaching. He came and greeted his guests. He saw her standing back near the tent and signalled to her. She came, tall and elegant, with her slow graceful walk, glad that she had oiled herself and put on clean garments. There was undisguised admiration in the eyes of the men. Abram saw it too.

Many years ago, Abram had foreseen that his wife's beauty might not only attract unwanted attention, but might even put him in jeopardy. One day he had light-heartedly discussed with her a plan for just such a contingency. He would say that she was his sister, not his wife. Then he would not be seen as the threatening, suspicious husband who might have to be eliminated. At least it could buy them some time. Sarai had laughed at the time and never really taken it seriously. She did not remember it, but he did, and kept it like a trick up his sleeve. It entered his head that now might be a good time to employ it.

He put out his hand and drew Sarai towards him and presented her to them. She was astonished to hear him say, 'May I introduce my sister to you? Her name is Sarai.'

The two Egyptians glanced at each other from under lowered lids, and nodded imperceptibly. They turned polite faces to Abram and Eliezer, and the ritual of hospitality progressed. A lamb was killed and dressed, and Sarai went to supervise its cooking. Abram plied his guests with wine and learned that they were officials in the court of Pharaoh, the title given to the Egyptian despot. Scouts had carried news to them of the arrival of a stranger with a considerable company of people and flocks and herds, evidently a man of substance! They had come to discover the identity of the traveller and to bring greetings from Pharaoh and offer their poor hospitality and shelter.

Abram knew very well that they had come to ascertain who he was, and what his intentions were. Did he come in peace or with more sinister objectives? Was he on his own or was he in league with another more powerful force? Thus the verbal fencing went on, but as the wine flowed and the delicious dishes of lamb and herbs and fruits appeared, tongues were loosened and everyone became more genial and relaxed.

Sarai herself served their guests and received their compliments on the food with quiet dignity. They were obviously taken with her beauty. Her smile was friendly, but she carried herself with a serene composure that was intriguing. She

certainly did not betray the inner turmoil that was raging at
her husband's strange introduction. Eventually the two men
made ready to leave and called to their servants to bring the
chariots nearer. They thanked Abram for his hospitality and
said they would be glad to return it. Pharaoh, they knew,
would welcome them heartily to the palace. Would Abram
do him the honour of bringing his sister to visit him? Abram
assented and the two men said they would send word in due
course. Then, with much courtesy on both sides, they took
their leave, driving off into the dusk in a swirl of dust and jin-
gling harnesses.

Abram delayed going into his tent as long as possible.
Eventually he crept in, hoping that Sarai was asleep. She was
not. She was waiting for him, puzzled and furious. 'Why did
you not own me as your wife?' she demanded. 'This afternoon you were full of compliments to me, saying how proud
you were of me, that I am still beautiful to you! Now you will
not even own me as your wife, but pass me off as your sister!
What have I done?' Then another thought assailed her. 'Or
what have I not done? It is because I am childless, is it not? I
am beautiful to look at, but I am not a proper wife! Is that
it?'

Her voice was rising hysterically. If he was disposed to be
gentle before, Abram now found himself hardening in his
attitude. Roughly he grasped her wrists and forced her down
on the bed. 'Be quiet!' he commanded sternly. She shrank
away and sat on the pillow, her hands locked round her
knees. Her hair tumbled down round her bent head. 'Listen,
woman! It is because you are beautiful that you put me in an
awkward position! Look at it this way: we are entering a land
we have never been in before, and we hear that the Egyptians
are a strange unpredictable lot. They could rush in here and
throw a spear through me and carry you off because they
fancy you. I am just playing a cautious game to keep them

off, to give us time to see how they behave. If they think you are just my sister, they are more likely to let me live. Anyway, we agreed to use this idea years ago. And it is partly true – we are related!'

Sarai had forgotten the proposed deceit and had never entertained it as a serious plan. She could not follow his warped logic. He seemed to think he would be safer if the Egyptians thought she was his sister, but what about her? He might save his own skin, but would it not expose her to danger? Falteringly she tried to explain this to him, but he was adamant that this was the best plan, and anyway, he was already committed to it now; those two men were probably even now telling Pharaoh about their visit!

'Do not disobey me in this!' he insisted. 'Besides, what I have said is partly true, for you are my half-sister!'[1] Sarai knew that the marriage relationship was the primary one and took precedence over any previous relationship. She was known and treated as his wife. And as his wife she must respect and obey him.

Drained and tired, she could not argue any more. She turned her face to the wall and shut her eyes. But sleep would not come. She felt used, devalued. She was not being honoured as a wife; she was being used as a screen to shield a man who was too cowardly to protect himself. She was shocked that her husband whom she had always admired and looked up to should employ such underhand tactics. She was desperately hurt that rather than protect her from possible danger his first thought was to save his own skin.

That night, Abram fell off his pedestal in her eyes. He was

---

[1] It is possible that they shared the same father, although this is not spoken of in the account of Terah's family tree in Genesis 11. Sarah may have been Terah's adopted daughter. Another suggestion is that she and Abram had the same grandparents and thus were cousins.

no longer her hero. He was a weak silly man, open to deception, motivated by self-preservation, willing to put another,
even his wife, in jeopardy. But he was still the man who
carried God's promise! Sarai found this very confusing. How
could God choose a man who was weak and vulnerable to
bring about his purposes?

*   *   *

Of course Sarah was not the last person to ask that question.
The truth is that there are no other sorts of human being for
God to use! All human beings, male and female, are weak
and fallible. If God chose people on their merits, because of
their strengths and accomplishments, there would be reason
for them to boast. As it is, no one can stand before God and
boast, because all that we achieve is by his grace alone. Every
person who enters his kingdom and his purposes is a self-
seeking, fearful, sin-prone human being. The fact that anything is ever done at all is remarkable. It is actually God who
does it, but because of his amazing kindness he shares the
labour, the pain, the fun, the joy and the glory with us – and
then calls us his co-workers! What a God of grace!

Sarah lived with a man who was fallible, foolish and frail,
yet who had the promises of God branded into his life. He
was a marked man! In him were embodied God's blessings
to the world!

We are told in the New Testament (1 Peter 3:6) that we
should see Sarah as a model for the way she respected her
husband. So it must have been that although Abraham used
her in this way she came to a decision to continue to honour
him and regard him as her 'lord'. Peter goes on to say that
we will be her daughters if we too submit to our husbands,
and then he adds a potent little phrase: '. . . do not give way
to fear'.

How strange! Here is a woman who is being asked to lie

about her identity in order to protect her husband. He is, in essence, abusing her trust. Surely in those circumstances she could be justified in thinking, 'That's the last time I listen to him, and as for obeying, forget it!' But what did she do? I believe that she made a decision to do what he required, but in faith that there was a higher authority than he watching over her. If God had indeed promised them not only a land but a son, then Abraham would survive and so would she.

*   *   *

'What will happen to me?' was the question dominating Sarai's thoughts as she and Abram were conducted into the presence of the Pharaoh. The muscular Egyptian bearers gently lowered the ornate litter with its silken cushions to the ground, and a broad arm steadied her as she rose to her feet. Then they were led up wide steps and through a great door, into the cool, cavernous chambers of the palace. As they passed through one splendid room after another, Abram and Sarai were a little overawed at such grandeur. Eventually they came into the great pillared throne room and were presented to the mighty Pharaoh. He received them graciously, and descended the steps from his throne. They all went into an adjoining apartment where a magnificent meal was laid out.

They were treated with the greatest respect and courtesy. There were other women present – servants, and women of Pharaoh's harem. Sarai's fair honey-coloured skin was in contrast to the darker skin of these women, and her cool elegance in her richly coloured and patterned robe kept from her days in Mesopotamia set her apart from them. They obviously admired her style. The Pharaoh's eyes were constantly flickering in her direction, although he maintained courteous attention to Abram.

The two courtiers who had visited Abram's camp were

also present and were watching everything closely. Pharaoh lifted a hand and beckoned one of them to his side. The courtier left, and moments later reappeared, followed by two servants carrying rolls of the finest pleated cotton gauze, such as the ladies of high rank were wearing. The other had a box containing a beautiful necklace made of rows of turquoise beads and pearls. They bowed low before Sarai, who sat up straight in surprise. The Pharaoh smiled at her, and leaned over his wine goblet to Abram. 'I beg your sister to receive these humble gifts,' he said. 'She is as fair as the moon.'

In her consternation Sarai's admired complexion flushed becomingly, and as her eyes looked for Abram, seeking help, she looked more beautiful than ever. He nodded to her, indicating that she should receive the gifts. She stood and walked slowly and gracefully to stand in front of Pharaoh and abased herself before him. She rose and thanked him prettily for his attention. Now he was not only admiring her looks but was captivated by her voice and her different way of speaking, for she and Abram spoke with an unusual accent.

Soon he had her seated by his side. He was evidently pleased by her appearance, but now also by her manner and her conversation. He called one of the women over and gave her an instruction. She bowed to Sarai and held out her hand. Then she and the other women bore her off with them.

Sarai at first assumed that they were merely showing her the women's quarters, but time went by and she began to realise that a small but beautiful chamber into which she was shown was set apart for her . . . and for who else? Now she began to understand the giggles and glances of the voluptuous girls who had brought her here; the significance of the sumptuous cushions and curtains, the floaty almost transparent gown draped across the bed. They intended her to stay! This lovely apartment was in fact a prison.

Later she discovered that Pharaoh had turned to Abram and spoken imperiously: 'I like your sister! She pleases me very much. I intend to take her into my household!' It was not a request but a statement that invited no discussion. Pharaoh then left the banqueting chamber and Abram was escorted politely but firmly to the door and sent home.

Sarai was now alone in the harem of a man who collected women as ornaments, like another man might collect gems or sculptures. What would happen to her? Her heart beat fast, and in spite of the stifling, perfumed air in the enclosed chamber, her hands were icy cold. Her eyes darted round the room, seeking any way of escape. Too late: a footfall outside, voices, a curtain drawn aside; Pharaoh himself standing in front of her; her trembling hand now in his, and being carried to his lips; his hands now at her shoulders, pushing off the cloaking outer garment; now at her waist untying the wide embroidered sash; now caressing her cheek, her neck, murmuring endearments about her velvet skin. She shook her hair over her face in her terror and confusion, and he laughed and forced her towards the bed, pulling at her shift until she lay there, exposed, vulnerable in her soft paleness. Her eyes were closed; she was tense, waiting for the next, too intimate, move. Nothing.

Sarai opened her eyes warily. Pharaoh had turned away, his hand clutching his belly and a grimace of pain distorting his face. He sat down heavily on the bed and sweat began to break out on his brow. He called hoarsely and a servant came in with a large brass bowl. The mighty Pharaoh leaned over and vomited into it.

Sarai moved away and grabbed her cloak and covered herself. Pharaoh was now lying on the bed breathing heavily, while servants hovered around worriedly. After a while he rose shakily to his feet and whispered his apologies. Then leaning on the arm of a servant, he tottered from the room.

Sarai lay down, shaking. It was some time before she was calm. Her last thought before she drifted off into an exhausted and troubled sleep was that Pharaoh was just like any other man who had overeaten at a feast. At least her ordeal was now postponed.

But it appeared that it was not just a case of over-indulgence, for the sickness swept through the palace. Sarai's needs were attended to by a darkly pretty little Egyptian maid called Hagar, who kept her informed of what was going on. It appeared that all over the palace people were going down with acute pains and vomiting. Sarai decided she was better off staying where she was out of harm's way. She instructed Hagar to bring her food that she was familiar with, plain and unadorned. She remained healthy.

A few days later she was summoned to Pharaoh. He received her in his personal apartments, but did not come near her or touch her. He looked weak and pale but assured her that he was recovering. 'I have had a dream,' he told her. 'A shining being came to me and told me that I am under a curse for taking another man's wife.' He looked at her gravely. 'Perhaps it was your God. I have made enquiries of the man I thought was your brother, and now I know he is really your husband.' He sighed heavily and passed a hand over his forehead. 'Why did he say that you were his sister?'

She opened her mouth to reply, but he made a gesture that forestalled her and said, ' No, don't say anything. I can only suppose that he had his reasons. Your God evidently highly regards him that he would protect you in this way. He must be a man of greater significance than I thought. He is coming to take you away now.' She thought she could detect fear in his eyes.

At this point Abram was led into the room. Pharaoh did not rise from his seat. He regarded Abram nervously. 'Why did you tell me that this woman was your sister when she is your wife?' he demanded querulously. 'I have suffered greatly because of her! Yes, and the rest of my household also! Now please take her and go! Pray to your God for me, but do not stay in my country. We want no more plagues and sickness!' He sank back on his cushioned seat, panting slightly, and a servant held a jewelled cup out to him. He took it and waved Abram and Sarai out of his sight.

Abram and Sarai were conducted under armed escort to their camp. Sarai was surprised to see many more sheep, cattle and camels than they had had before – gifts from Pharaoh when she had been taken into the harem. They struck camp and early next day were on the move once again, this time north-east, back towards Canaan.

*　　*　　*

How did this odd husband and wife now behave towards one another? We shall see as we continue the story that each was far from perfect. It is a strange interlude that is difficult for us to understand, coming from a culture that is so distant in time and in practice. Yet here it is recorded for us, unvarnished and distasteful. How embarrassing that these patriarchal figures behaved in this way! We want to be men and women of faith, to be obedient, to have that pilgrim mentality that embraces sacrifice, is willing to leave the safety of home and plunge into the unknown, believing the promises of God!

'Oh, yes,' we say, 'I want to be like Abraham; I want to be like Sarah.' And then they go and act like this! Fortunately the Bible is very specific in the things we are to emulate in Abraham and Sarah. In Isaiah 51:1–2 it is faith in multiplication. In Romans 4:13–23 it is righteousness through faith. In Hebrews, 11:8–12 it is obedience and vision. In 1 Peter 3:5–6 it is a submissive spirit. The Bible certainly does not want us to see them as a role model for cowardice, selfishness and manipulative behaviour! But neither does it whitewash its heroes and heroines. The Bible is full of people with human weakness. The grace of God is shown over and over again in his amazing kindness in choosing ordinary men and women to work with him to bring about his purposes on the earth. Even when they fall and stumble, he does not abandon them and revert to plan B; there is no plan B. He picks them up, brings them back in, and continues where they left off.

The Bible is also very clear about principles. The New Testament enunciates more explicitly the principle of submission that is latent in the Old Testament. Sarah is commended as an example of a wife who submitted to her husband 'without giving way to fear'. Abraham abused her trust and her obedience to him. He exploited her to protect himself. Disgraceful – reason enough to ditch the entire principle! Except she did not see it that way.

Why not? Was she a doormat – a weak and feeble thing who was so conditioned by her culture that she had no strength to stand up for herself? We shall see that she certainly was not a woman who was afraid of her husband, or above taking initiatives or even bending him to her will when it suited her. Sarah was a strong woman.

I believe that 'without giving way to fear' is a significant phrase. Peter says that she was a godly woman; the only person she feared was God. If God wanted her to respect her husband and bow to his wishes, she would, as an expression of her devotion and obedience to God. Ultimately that's where her obedience was directed. She believed that Abraham's poor example of headship did not negate the principle. God saw the attitude of her heart and honoured her for it. (More on this in Chapter 12.)

Maybe Abraham did indeed fall off the pedestal, but God does not want women only to honour their husbands if they conform to their image of what they should be. He wants

them to respect them because God tells them to. In fact their
obedience in this may well be a factor in helping them
become the men they should be; to be affirmed in their mas-
culinity, to gain self-respect, and learn confidence and
responsibility in their leadership roles.

I wonder if it was a chastened Abraham who fetched his
mistreated wife. I wonder if it was an irate and hurt Sarah
who rejoined him. Although they were by now a couple of
many years' standing they still had many more adventures
and tests to go through. Like us, as they muddled along they
learned many things about each other and about God. They
made more mistakes, but eventually God's purposes did
come to pass. Their failures were swallowed up in his success;
and their success is still celebrated. 'God is not ashamed to
be called their God' (Hebrews 11:16).

8

Hagar

Sarai leaned against the doorpost of the tent. The rocky landscape before her was dominated by a massive oak tree, around which the black tents were clustered. Nearby was a well, and sheep-folds were not far distant. The air was filled with the bleating of ewes and new-born lambs. The shepherds were kept busy these spring days and nights! Flowers clothed the hills and a pair of doves was cooing in the branches of the oak.

It seemed to Sarai's sad eyes that new life was burgeoning all around, but her arms, her womb and her heart were empty. She was tired with a tiredness that was not just the physical fatigue of ten years of wandering. Her bones certainly ached more these days, and everything she did took more effort, but the ache in her heart wearied her more than the ache in her bones.

She was glad that they had remained more or less settled in this spot not far from Hebron for several months now. It had become something of a base for Abram's household. After leaving Egypt they had made their way slowly back to Canaan. The pace was slowed down because they had by now become a very large company. Both Abram's and Lot's flocks had flourished in Egypt, and Pharaoh, in his initial display of goodwill to Abram because of his admiration for Sarai, had added further to his livestock. Abram had left Egypt a wealthy man. Not only sheep, cattle and camels had increased his possessions, but he had also acquired much gold and jewellery, and his retinue included more servants, male and female.

In fact the company had become so numerous that conflict was constantly breaking out among the shepherds of Abram and Lot as they vied for pasture and water for their multiplying flocks. Life became so fraught with their quarrelling that Lot and Abram agreed to part. Lot had gone towards the luscious Jordan Valley to the east and Abram remained on the hills west of the Jordan and the Salt Sea.

One of the servants they had taken with them from Egypt was Hagar, the attractive little Egyptian maid who had served Sarai so well in Pharaoh's palace. Pharaoh had been so eager to speed their departure that he conceded practically anything they wanted, as long as they would leave! Sarai asked for Hagar and she came willingly. The bond between them deepened, and she became Sarai's trusted personal maid and companion. After years of travelling with Lot's family, Sarai missed them when they departed. She had become fond of Lot's wife and had been a loving great-aunt to her two little girls. So Hagar now became her main confidante.

Broodingly she looked over towards the east and thought of Lot's wife now and wondered how the girls were. How were they faring down there in the valley near the town of Sodom? She shivered slightly, remembering a time when they had all been travelling near there and had camped for a while. Some of the men had come out to meet them, and she remembered their bold lascivious eyes when they rested on Lot's pretty daughters, and their loose conversation.

'I hope Lot is able to protect his household well,' she

murmured doubtfully to herself. He was a good man, but weak. He knew what was right, but tended to take the easy path. She shook her head, knowing his easygoing, undisciplined lifestyle and procrastinating ways. 'Those pretty little daughters of his are going to be a handful,' she told herself. Their mother was even less decisive than their father, and their household was likely to be a fairly ramshackle affair – quite a contrast to the smoothly run, efficient camp of Abram.

She shook her head again, but this time it was not over the wayward family in the valley, but in exasperation at herself. 'Great-aunt!' she almost spat the words out. 'I should be a grandmother by now!' Irritably she called for a stool and sat down in the shade. She could see most of the settlement from here and idly watched the comings and goings of the shepherds and servants. Vaguely she wondered where Hagar was. Perhaps she had gone to see some of the new-born lambs.

Lambs! Even that thought brought a renewal of the sharp pain in her heart, and her shoulders sagged with the weight of grief. Her tiredness was the heaviness that comes from the disappointment of unfulfilled dreams; the crushing sense of disillusionment when one has allowed one's hopes to rise high . . . and then waited . . . and waited . . . and waited, it seemed, in vain. Now she had to face the unasked question: 'Was it all a mistake? A self-inflicted dream? The product of wishful thinking? Did we really hear God?' For in all reality she could never have a baby now.

And that was how Abram found her: sitting forlornly under the oak tree, with spring all around her, but a tear trickling down her cheek. He fetched another stool and sat down beside her, and wiped the tear with his finger. Then he took her hand and traced the lines in the palm and kissed it. She put her other hand over his and wordlessly they clung together, each knowing the pain that the other carried, but unable to express it in words. Then, 'I am afraid, Abram,' she whispered. 'If we got it wrong about the baby, did we get everything else wrong as well?'

Abram realised that she was in a vortex of despair, and tried to reassure her that it was indeed God who had led them to this land. But she was only half-listening. At length, he looked up and realised that Eliezer was hovering nearby. He beckoned him over, and Eliezer's trusting face warmed his heart. The young man squatted down by him and began to talk of the fast arrival of the many lambs.

'I'm going back over there now,' he said, gesturing to the hills beyond. 'They need as many hands as possible right now!'

Abram patted his shoulder affectionately. 'I think I'll come with you,' he announced impulsively. 'Wait while I get my stick and cloak!' As he turned to go into the tent, Hagar appeared, striking in a crimson robe, her riotous dark curls tumbling around her shoulders. Sarai noticed wryly how both men, the old as well as the younger, smiled at her and made laughing comments. Hagar went into the tent and fetched Abram's cloak and stick for him.

Dully, Sarai watched the two men stride off together. What she did not know was that all through that busy evening and into the night, her words kept coming back to Abram: 'I am afraid . . . was it God?'

She knew that it was hard work delivering the lambs. Some of the ewes delivered their offspring fairly easily, but some needed help, especially if they were giving birth to twins or triplets and the tiny creatures were all tangled up inside the mother. The shepherds went around the grunting, straining mothers, their skilful hands disentangling the little bodies and pulling them out. Every so often a relieved and delighted laugh could be heard as another lamb rolled onto

the straw and then tottered to its legs and found its way to
the mother's teats.

Usually a couple of men would put up a makeshift shelter
of branches and rocks, but it would be well past midnight
before anyone could snatch a few hours' sleep. She knew that
Abram would be exhausted when he entered the shelter and
rolled himself in his cloak. The nights were chilly on the bare
hills.

Later, he told her how suddenly a light shone in his
dreams. A voice he was learning to recognise spoke: 'Do not
be afraid, Abram.'

He was on his knees, waiting.

'I am your shield, your very great reward.'

Humbly, simply, he dared to reply, 'O Sovereign Lord, I
remain childless. The one who will inherit my estate is Eliezer
of Damascus. You have given me no children, so my servant
will be my heir.'

Then the word of the Lord came to him: 'This man will
not be your heir, but a son coming from your own body will
be your heir.'

The brightness faded, and Abram sat up, rubbing his eyes.
Every word that he had heard was crystal clear in his mind.
His heart was thumping and an awe was upon him. He sat
still, hardly daring to breathe. A great presence filled the tiny
shelter. He felt he must go outside. Slowly, carefully, so as
not to disturb the others, but also like a drunk man who
picks his way with exaggerated care, he groped his way to the
door.

Outside, the cold air hit him in the face. He gasped, eyes
wide open, dazzled, afraid with a different fear now. The
presence was everywhere, filling the star-bright heavens, the
shadowy hills, the hollows in the rocks, pressing him down
into the damp grass.

'Look up!' the voice commanded. He lay on his back and

gazed at the millions of stars dusting the velvety sky. Their numbers and their brilliance overwhelmed him.

'Count them!'

He began. After a few minutes, he began again. It was an impossible task. He felt the divine laughter. Then softly he heard, 'So shall your offspring be.'

'I believe you, Lord.' He stretched out his arms where he lay and said it again: 'I believe you, Lord.' He stood to his feet and said it loudly and deliberately: 'I believe you, Lord!'

Faith was born as he believed in his heart and confessed with his mouth the word of God;[1] and God heard and said, 'My servant is righteous.'[2]

Abram began to walk about, enjoying this conversation with God. It was like talking to a friend! The next thing his friend said was, 'It was I, you know, who brought you out of Ur of the Chaldeans. I intend to give you this land.'

Abram felt that he was now in a new phase of his relationship with God. They were talking together and he could ask questions. 'How can I know?' he asked.

Then God told him to fetch a heifer, a goat, a ram, a dove and a pigeon. So the next evening Abram was waiting, with the carcasses arranged as he had been instructed. He had had a disturbed night and a busy day fighting off predators, and as the sun was setting he fell into a deep sleep. While he slept, the presence of God enveloped him again, thick and strong and terrifying. Weak and helpless in his grip, he heard what would happen to the nation that would come from his own loins. They would be strangers in another country and enslaved for 400 years, but would come out with great possessions, back to this land.

Abram lay prostrate in wonder and terror as God ratified

---

[1] Romans 10:9–10
[2] Genesis 15:6

the covenant with fire. When he was able, he left the smoking remains of the dead animals and shakily made his way back to the camp. He must find Sarai.

Sarai had not seen her husband for two days and nights since he had gone with Eliezer to the lambing. She had had plenty of time to think and now she had come to a decision.

Hagar had been watching the new-born lambs, and had returned to her mistress with amusing anecdotes of their playfulness: how they skipped about and butted their demanding little heads at their mothers' udders, and how the mothers knew their own lambs and were not fooled when a stray one tried to wheedle its way in. Sarai encouraged her chatter, finding that it distracted her from her despondency. She enjoyed Hagar's bright cheerfulness.

The girl had grown into a graceful young woman. Her thin young body had filled out ripely, and her thick curly hair hung down nearly to her waist. As she talked, glad that her sad mistress was responding to her efforts to cheer her up, her large and brilliant black eyes lit up her expressive face. She moved around the tent, straightening, tidying, picking things up, folding clothes, her movements quick and deft. Sarai knew that many of the shepherds and servants watched her hungrily, but she had so far deflected their advances with a careless toss of her head and light, teasing banter that they found tantalising.

She was so attractive, Sarai thought. How long would she be content to confine herself to serving her mistress? She should get a man, have children! And then an idea began to form in her mind. What better man than one who had the blessing of God on his life? One who had promises about being a father of a multitude? And here was a woman who was ready for child-bearing; who was warm and ripe, sturdy and robust. She would make a good mother. Fertility was written all over her!

Sarai looked down at her own body. She knew she was comely enough to retain her husband's affection; tall, slim and shapely still, she knew he desired her. But she was dead within: her womb was dried up, and all promise of life was finished. Yet there must be a child! There must! Her arms ached to hold a baby. Surely God could not be so cruel as to mock her, to promise a baby and then leave her with an aching void! There must be another way!

God had made the promise, but God, seemingly, had not equipped her to bring forth life. So he must mean her to do it another way. It must be God who had brought Hagar into their life. Sarai had not menstruated now for several years. She was finished, barren, withered, dead. This was the end of her hopes and dreams. Face facts, woman! Stop being sentimental and unreal! God has forgotten an old has-been like you! Find another way! Oh! Surprise, surprise – here *is* another way! Must be God. Let's help him out.

How was she going to sell this to her righteous husband? She went to meet him. Here he was coming down the hillside, fresh from a major meeting with God, eager to share with his beloved wife God's renewed promises. He remembered her despair and longed to tell her how God had spoken to him in the night under the stars. 'Don't be afraid . . .' It wasn't too late. He hadn't forgotten. His promise still stood. Keep believing . . . Not just a baby, but a whole nation would come from their union. Excited, he hastened his steps. There she was, coming towards him!

They met. Sarai spoke first. Trembling, she took a deep breath. 'Abram: listen! I've been thinking. I cannot have children. My body has ceased to function. It is impossible . . .' Quickly Abram cut in. He put his hand gently across her mouth, not wanting to hear her despairing tone. He was buoyant in faith, fresh from hearing the renewed promises of God.

'Wait, Sarai!' he urged. 'Let me tell you what happened to me last night. As you know, I went to help with the lambing, and I slept in one of the booths the men had set up. In the middle of the night, the Lord God came to me again and assured me that a son would be born from my own body. I had settled for Eliezer being my heir. But no! I shall have an heir who is my own flesh and blood!' He turned a glowing face to her. 'It will happen, Sarai! It will!'

Her pain-filled eyes searched his face. 'Did he mention the mother?' she whispered, her voice constricting as she forced the words out.

Abram felt all the wind knocked out of him. He stared at her dumbly. 'What do you mean?'

'I mean, you are to be the father, but who is to be the mother?' she said desperately.

'Why, you of course,' he answered quickly.

'Is that what he said? Did he mention my name? Did he say you would have the child through me? Abram? Did he?'

He was disconcerted. 'Well, not in so many words, no . . . but surely, Sarai, that is what he meant! I mean, who else?' He suddenly found himself floundering, unsure, trying to remember the exact words of the message he had heard. Now that Sarai pressed him, all he could remember was that God had promised that a son coming from his own body would be his heir. He was beginning to feel confused. He tried to recover his confident mood. 'It must be you!' he repeated.

She stared up at him, and her pain was like a jagged torturing thing. Her eyes swam with tears and dripped over. 'I can't, Abram. I can't!' she gasped between sobs. 'It's impossible. It can't be me. It can't be me.'

'But God said . . .' he began again.

She interrupted. 'I know God said!' She was almost angry. 'God said you would have a son. And it is very important

that you have a son because you have to found a new family.
You are to be the head of a new clan, a nation! I don't dispute
that. But what I would like to know is, how is this going to
be achieved? Because it can't happen through me.' She wept
afresh. 'We have tried and tried, and now it is too late.'

Abram gazed sadly at the ground and pushed a pebble
round in the dust with his toe. He was in a quandary. He had
thought that Sarai would have risen as he had to the renewed
promise, but he could see that she was not in that place of
faith. Moreover, what she was saying was indisputable. They
turned and walked back together to the tent.

They sat together in the shade and Sarai's sobs gradually
subsided. After a while, she sat up resolutely and turned to
face Abram. 'It's been ten years since we came here,' she said,
trying to sound reasonable and matter-of-fact. 'We came
because we believed that God called us – well, called *you* –
and that he would found a new nation through you. I have
willingly come with you as you know, and I will do whatever
I can to facilitate God's plan. But this – bearing a child – I
cannot do.' The tears threatened again but she ploughed on.
'But there may be another way.' He was listening intently.
She found it so hard to say the next thing, so she said it
quickly. 'You could sleep with Hagar, my maid. Perhaps we
can build a family through her.' It was out now; it could not
be recalled.

Abram was in turmoil, speechless. He was robbed of the
initiative. Suddenly an idea was being brought to him and he
was not in the lead any more. He was face to face with stark
reality. God had said he would have a son. His wife could not
produce that son, so they would have to use another way.
Hagar was available. God had not blessed his union with
Sarai, but another woman was at hand.

But how could he ignore the wife of his youth and sleep
with another? Could that be God's way? Surely not! But how

else was he going to produce the promised heir? Surely in this case the end justified the means?

Hagar appeared round the corner. She smiled at him, her mouth wide and full-lipped, and her eyes alive and sparkling. She walked by, her skirts swinging with her hips. There was a vibrant sense of youth and vitality. He stared after her for a moment.

When he turned back to face Sarai, she was watching him. A sudden desolation swept over him. He felt unsure of everything. Was this really all about fulfilling the promises of God? Or was it about gratifying those deep maternal longings? Did God need their help? Was this the only way?

'I don't know,' he muttered.

But Sarai talked on: talked of her inability, of Hagar's availability, and of how important it was that this family was begun. 'How much longer must we wait?' she finished.

Abram was persuaded. He would do it. 'You talk to her,' he said.

He went off to inspect a horse that Pharaoh had given him. It was in foal. Everywhere he looked there was pregnancy and fertility! He felt bemused and uneasy. The joyous intimacy he had enjoyed with God last night had trickled away.

Sarai called for Hagar and they had a long and confidential discussion. As Sarai had suspected, she did not find her maid hard to convince. 'I am yours, mistress,' she murmured. 'I will do whatever you think best.' But her brilliant black eyes, though meekly downcast, gleamed even brighter, and a secret smile curved her lips.

That night, two shadowy figures entered the tent where Abram lay in pent-up anticipation. Sarai led the Egyptian girl in by the hand, and took her through the partition to the sleeping quarters. 'She is yours,' was all she said, then withdrew into the night. It was the hardest thing she had ever done, and she had never felt so alone as she went to her own empty bed.

*   *   *

How *could* she? And how could *he*? But desperation is a powerful feeling and resorts to many plausible means to be alleviated. Sarah was in the grip of a deep despair arising from the belief that she could not have children, and all the conflicting emotions that went with that. The sense of failure arising from a culture that honoured the ability to give birth as a means of validating personhood; the pain of personal loss, the empty arms, the unfulfilled maternal instinct; and the heavy bitter feeling of having been let down – all demanded relief.

But more than that, I believe that she wanted to see the promises of God come about and she had grown weary of waiting. What could she do to hurry things along? Her arguments were so plausible! God had said . . . she was barren . . . here was another woman . . . she could have the baby . . . God's will is done! Or is it? God's will would be Isaac, but the result was Ishmael.

People can grow sad and frustrated as they wait – interminably, it seems – for something they feel God has promised. A girl may long for a husband, and she knows she should marry a Christian, but a Christian man never seems to come along who wants to marry her, and time is passing by! She is beginning to feel a little desperate. Then she meets someone who is kind and friendly; they enjoy each other's company, seem to have so much in common. She realises she is falling in love. A little voice reminds her, 'He is not a Christian,' and loving friends warn her. But she makes her decision and marries him, because she cannot wait any longer for a Christian man who never appears! This one came along: it must be God's will, she persuades herself.

How many of us have met sad, disillusioned women, trapped in marriages where their partner does not share their faith? On the other hand, there are women who waited patiently, refusing to be sucked into relationships out of expediency, who have found happiness with a Christian man who suddenly came on the scene in later years when they had virtually given up hope.

A similar situation can confront those in the realm of business. A crisis threatens, and then a solution appears to offer itself. The trouble is, there are aspects of it that prick the conscience. They are uneasily aware that if they take this option they will be compromising principles of honesty and integrity. But things become pressing, so they suppress conscience and make the deal, even though they belong to a God who has promised us that he will honour those who honour him. And at first they seem justified in their choices, but later down the track, when the deal becomes exposed, they know they cannot call on God to vindicate them, since they went against his will in the first place!

When we take matters into our own hands out of frustration, fear or impatience, our hands are tied when we get into difficulties. We have to live with the consequences of our actions. Often it is very hard to wait and keep believing that God will honour his word, but we believe in one who has promised to help 'in time of need', or 'in the nick of time'.

Hagar epitomises the pragmatic approach. The promise on its own was not enough for Sarah. It did not appear to be working, so she would use whatever else was at hand that had the potential to get the job done. We must be clear that just as Abraham could rely on the promise of God and find him faithful, so can we continue to put our trust in the word of God.

On a wider scale, Hagar can stand for efforts of Christian people who have given up on the church. God's strategy for implementing the rule and reign of Jesus is, and always has been, the church. Jesus has been made head over all things – for the church. The trouble is that many Christian people have given up on the church. To them, she is a dried-up, withered old has-been. She has no power to bring forth life. Yet the God-given urge to reproduce is still in them. What are they going to do with it? Through the gospel they have been given living seed, yet the church does not seem to be a very promising womb to put it in. So they look for a surrogate mother. This is why, I believe, many organisations spring up, from the very best of intentions, which ignore the church.

But, you may say, they must be of God, because he seems to bless them. People get saved, cleaned up, healed and changed in movements other than the church. But then the seed, the gospel, is potent; it has life and the ability to bring forth life. And God's grace is such that whosoever calls on the name of the Lord will be saved, however imperfect the medium. God has established a creative principle: plant a seed and it will grow. Paul was able to say that he rejoiced that the gospel was preached, even if it was preached by rivals with the wrong motives! It was still powerful, and the only means of salvation. So yes, even outside the church the gospel will 'work'.

But God's best is the plan he set in motion right back at the beginning with Abraham. It is that he should have a people for his very own possession, a people of promise. Abraham is the head of this family, the first-born of many brethren. We collectively are the dwelling place of God in the Spirit.

If you think the church is boring, it may be because you have never understood the beauty of it, the wonder of our monogamous God who is totally committed to his bride, and to bringing her to fruitful maturity! Perhaps you have only seen a pathetic travesty of the church: grey, dull, lifeless, solemn and joyless, racked with disputes, inward-looking, concerned with triviality and unconcerned with showing the world the mercy and love of God. How can you put all your energies into that? And especially, how can you expect people to be born again in that?

What a tragedy when the church should be vibrant with the overflowing life of the Spirit, moving in authority under the anointed authority that God has appointed! That is why the restoration of the church has become such an urgent issue. There is much fruit to be born, but to truly bring honour to the Father, it must be born in the right way: through the bride.

9

The God Who Sees

The next morning, Hagar was late coming into Sarai's tent to serve her as she usually did. Sarai was up and dressed, tidying the bedding when Hagar sauntered in yawning. Sarai looked at her sharply. Many questions hovered on her tongue, but she kept her mouth shut. A change had taken place in their relationship. Gradually she perceived that Hagar was assuming a different status now. Something she had not foreseen was happening. She had thought naïvely that everything would go on as before, except that eventually a child might be added into the mix. But now she began to suspect that though they might gain a child between them, she was about to lose a maid and a friend.

Hagar would not look her in the eye this morning. There was a different air about her, a defiance that was very disconcerting. She attended to her duties half-heartedly, almost unwillingly. When she dropped a bowl, Sarai spoke sharply: 'Hagar! Mind what you're doing!'

Hagar lifted her chin then, and looked Sarai full in the eye. A little mocking smile played around her mouth. With exaggerated care she placed the bowl on the shelf, then, still looking at Sarai, she swaggered out.

Sarai sat down on the couch, amazed and angry. 'How

dare she treat me like that! A mere servant! I am her mistress
. . .' Then she began to wonder: was she a 'mere servant' any
more? Technically speaking, she supposed she was now a
concubine. And how was a concubine to be treated? Oh dear,
this was going to be more complicated than she had bar-
gained for. It was becoming apparent to her that she had
been very naïve to think that in sleeping with her maid
Abram would be performing a merely biological act.
Something far more complex had taken place. He had been
joined to her and the whole balance of their relationship was
subtly altered.

Sarai never knew how many times Hagar slept with
Abram. She tried not to think about it; it was too painful.
But it was not long before the young woman conceived. One
morning Hagar did not appear at all. One of the other maids
went to look for her and came back with the news that
Hagar was lying on her bed feeling ill. Sarai's heart lurched
in her chest. She guessed that Hagar was pregnant, and
knew that she should go and talk to her, but she found
within herself a strange reluctance: she almost feared to
know the truth.

Later in the day she found the young woman going about
her duties with a listless, distracted air, and took her on one
side. Hagar answered her questions. Sure enough, there was
but one conclusion to come to: she was pregnant. Sarai did
not congratulate her or embrace her. She simply turned on
her heel and walked back to her tent.

She acknowledged to herself a conflict of emotions. Her
plan had worked; Abram was going to be a father. She
herself was going to be a mother – sort of. But she did not
feel elated. She felt usurped, passed over. That evening at the
meal-time, she watched Hagar closely. She noted the girl's
difficulty as the smell of the roast meat rose on the air.
Everyone else sniffed appreciatively, but Hagar turned away,

nauseated. Sarai felt unreasonably angry with her. Hagar should eat and be grateful, not turn away in disgust!

Hagar felt Sarai's eyes upon her and looked up. She lifted her chin and smiled slightly. Slowly, her eyes still locked on Sarai's, she put her hand on her stomach and gently patted it, as if to say, 'I have something very precious in here that you have never had.'

Sarai's mouth tightened and her hand clenched as impotent fury swept over her. From then on, Abram, Sarai and Hagar lived as an uncomfortable trio, a *ménage à trois* in which both women silently tried to establish their own superiority and Abram drifted miserably between them, aware of the dark undercurrents of jealousy and rivalry, but unable to bring resolution.

Soon it was common knowledge that Hagar was expecting a child. Curious eyes watched to see how Sarai reacted, and how Abram treated Hagar. The old hierarchy had been disrupted. Sarai was still wife number one, but Hagar, although only a concubine, was carrying a child and that gave her a new prestige that challenged Sarai's position. As Hagar's figure changed shape with the child growing in her womb, Sarai grew more and more paranoid with jealousy. Hagar was not subtle. She deliberately thrust out her stomach, exaggerated her condition by the clothes she wore and complained loudly of backache, headache, tiredness and nausea. One day in the kitchen, when Hagar declared she was too tired to help with chopping the vegetables, Sarai picked up a pan and banged it down on Hagar's head.

'Get out!' she screamed. 'Stop flouncing around in here with your big belly! Anyone would think no one had ever been pregnant before, the way you behave! Get out of my sight!' Hagar stared at her for a moment in shock, rubbing her head. Then she backed away fearfully and turned and ran out.

As luck would have it, she ran right into Abram. He caught sight of her frightened, tearful face, and grabbed her arm. 'What is going on?' he demanded anxiously. 'Has someone hurt you?' She clung to his arm, relieved to have his undivided attention. She missed his intimacy. Now that she was expecting the baby, her job was done. He no longer slept with her. She felt used and lonely. She sobbed and poured out her sorrow and the story of Sarai's abusive treatment.

Abram sucked in his breath. He was angry with Sarai, but he was annoyed with Hagar too. He did not love her as he loved Sarai, and he was not unaware of Hagar's indiscreet ways and the little calculated humiliations that she was constantly baiting Sarai with. Yet he owed her. She was carrying his child. She was entitled to some consideration. He sighed. Life was suddenly very complicated.

At that moment Sarai came to the tent door, and there before her was Abram, standing close to Hagar, his arm encircling her protectively while she sobbed on his shoulder. Her fury boiled over and her normal dignity, already seriously eroded, departed completely. Hands on hips, face distorted in fury, she exploded, all her pent-up frustration and feelings of failure and rejection erupting in a stream of unguarded language.

'Slut!' she raged at the Egyptian. 'You snake! You slithered in here among us and we sheltered you. Everything you have is ours, your food, your clothes, and now see what you have done, you little whore! You have usurped me, your benefactor! You queen it over me as if I were mud . . .'

Hysteria was rising as she directed her anger at Abram. 'I gave my maid to you,' she yelled. 'Now look what you've done! Look at her, swaggering about, thrusting out her belly! She is destroying us with her arrogance. And me? I suppose I am nothing around here. It's clear that is what *she* thinks. I gave her the chance to bear our child and she repays me with cheap jibes and insults. How can you put up with it? I am wronged and humiliated! Me, your wife! And you let her carry on – you encourage her. You both make me feel like dirt . . . it's not fair! God knows it isn't fair!' She ran out of steam and subsided, sobbing helplessly.

Abram was furious and ashamed. He pushed Hagar aside and glanced around, and noticed that they were now the centre of a circle of interested on-lookers. Sarai stood on one side, her grey hair falling down wildly, her wrinkled face streaked with tears; Hagar stood on the other, her body swollen with pregnancy, her face flushed and angry and a large bruise beginning to show on the side of her face where the pan had hit her. He was in the middle.

He groaned. Women! He went to Sarai and grasped her wrists. 'Sarai! Remember who you are! Compose yourself!' Her convulsive sobbing quietened to sniffs and hiccups. Irritably he yelled at the curious observers, 'Go away! Get on with your work!' Eliezer appeared and Abram told him to get rid of them. They shuffled off reluctantly and Abram was left with the two women. He felt embarrassed and helpless. Again he turned to Sarai, ignoring Hagar.

'Sarai . . .' He did not know what to say.

She interrupted, her lacerated emotions distorting her logic, finding refuge in self-pity and deluded self-righteousness. 'God knows I am despised,' she said tragically. 'Let him be the judge.' She drew herself up, rigid with hurt pride.

Abram felt his hands were tied. He knew that somewhere in her arguments there were serious flaws, but he had lost track. He was confused and weary of it all. Still ignoring Hagar, he did the best he could to give Sarai back her dignity.

'Do what you like,' he said. 'She's your maid. The problem is between the two of you. Sort it out!'

With that he turned on his heel and walked away,

abdicating completely any responsibility to arbitrate. Sarai and Hagar were left alone. Sarai knew she had thrown away her self-respect. Nevertheless, drawing the tattered remnants of her former dignity around her like an old cloak, she straightened her back, smoothed her hair and tried to act with disdainful unconcern. Hagar watched her nervously, still fingering the growing bump on her head.

'You!' Sarai spat out the word. 'Get back in that kitchen and don't let me catch you slacking again!' Then she stalked off to her tent without a backward glance.

The cold war had now become seriously hot. Daggers were drawn. However, Sarai now had the upper hand, and took every opportunity to make life hard for her rival. Hagar, vulnerable in her pregnancy, felt she had no champion to plead her cause. Abandoned and alone, she went about her chores with none of her former bravado. She tried to keep a low profile and avoid all contact with Sarai, but somehow her growing size, with its attendant clumsiness, seemed to infuriate her mistress. Her back ached and her legs swelled, but there was no relief from the daily round of tasks, and Sarai was adept at finding extra petty things for her to do, which prevented her from resting even though she felt so tired.

At night she lay on her pallet feeling the baby kicking inside her, but unable to share her emotions with the father or anyone else. She was desperately afraid of giving birth in this hostile environment; she felt used, alone and unloved. Sullen and miserable in the sleepless nights, unable to find a comfortable position, she wept quietly. If only she could get away! But where could she go? Could she find her way back to Egypt? Escape became her preoccupation. Day and night she thought about it. Perhaps if she could get as far as the main trade route through Shur, she could hitch up with a merchant caravan going to Egypt.

Then one evening, after a particularly gruelling day, she

decided she could bear no more. She rolled up a few possessions in a cloth and tied it in a bundle, and filled a skin with water. Then when everyone had retired for the night and all was quiet, she crept out of her tent and carefully made her way out of the camp. Her goal was to get past Hebron and onto the main trade route to Shur before dawn. Surely she could find a place to wait in safety! Camel trains were frequently going south, so she should not have to wait long.

At first all went according to plan. The moon was high and bright, and as she made her way as quickly as possible over the rocky ground, she felt almost elated. She reached Hebron and skirted round it and kept going in a southwesterly direction – at least she thought she did. But when daybreak came, all she could see was endless stony ridges in every direction. She was perturbed, but thought that soon she must come to the highway. She trudged on, while the sun climbed higher and beat down mercilessly. The horizon shimmered in the glaring heat and confused her.

She came across a cave and went in to find some shade and to rest. She drank sparingly from her water supply and ate some dates and bread from her bundle. Then, exhausted, she lay down and slept. It was late afternoon when she awoke. Fuzzy with sleep, and stiff from lying on the ground, she hauled herself to her feet and looked out of the cave. She could see from the sun that the day was far gone. Panicking slightly, she hurried out and walked rapidly in the direction that she thought was west. Eventually she would hit the track, surely! But she must keep going, because no caravan was ever going to find her here, and her food and water would not last for more than a day. She would cover as much distance as she could before nightfall.

But when nightfall came she had not yet reached an oasis or a track, or seen any merchants or any other sign of civilisation. She had seen a few mountain gazelles in the distance, and nearly stepped on a scorpion. When a snake slithered across her path, she cried out in fear, but there was no one to hear her.

The blackness of the night was unendurable. She found a crude refuge under some rocks, but her sleep was fitful, as little sounds disturbed her. She could not forget the snakes and lizards and scorpions, and imagined them slithering and scuttling all around her. It was bitterly cold too and her cloak was far from adequate to keep her warm.

At last daylight came. Never had a dawn been so welcome! She sat in the sun like a lizard, relishing the warmth soaking into her weary bones, and ate her last dates and bread, and drank some water. There was very little left now. She picked up her little bundle and began to walk purposefully. She would not panic. She would find water. Someone would come. She would find a road, a well, a group of nomads or shepherds.

She kept on. Around midday, she knew she had to rest and drink. She drank the last precious drops, and allowed herself a short rest, then doggedly went on. But soon, totally exhausted, unbearably thirsty, defeated by the furnace-like heat, she sank to the ground and lay there in utter despair. The baby kicked inside her, and a tear trickled down her hot face. She thought she would die, and the baby with her. She barely had strength to weep for this little life that would never see the light of day. She pulled her cloak over her head and lay inert, a pathetic heap on the burning sand.

A light touch on her shoulder, then a more determined shake. Water poured over her head, cool and refreshing. She thought she was dreaming. A strong arm lifted her shoulders and cradled her, while a bottle of water was thrust between her lips and a voice urged her, 'Drink! Drink!' She obeyed. Then the voice said, 'There is a spring nearby,' and half-led, half-carried her weak, limp form a little distance round some rocks and down a slope. At the bottom a small spring gushed out from under some large overhanging rocks.

She leaned over and slaked her head and face in its delicious depths and drank deeply. At last she sat back against a boulder, drew a long breath, and looked up at her benefactor. A man of the desert was kneeling beside her, a leather bag and a staff on the ground. Her eyes searched his face and saw there only friendly compassion. It seemed natural to reach out and grasp his hand as she said, 'You saved my life.'

His eyes nearly disappeared into the crinkles of his deeply tanned face as he smiled. 'Yes, Hagar,' he answered. Startled, she gazed at him open-mouthed. 'You are Hagar, maid to Sarai,' he stated matter-of-factly.

'How do you know?' she faltered.

'It is my business to know. Now, where have you come from and where are you going?'

It seemed pointless to enter into a long account of how ill-used she was, so she said simply, 'I am running away from my mistress.'

He looked hard at her and she dropped her gaze before those searching eyes. 'Go back to her and submit to her,' he said gently but firmly.

It was the last thing she wanted to hear. She twisted her fingers together, and shook her head. Who was this man? How did he know who she was? And how could he speak to her with such authority? She looked at him frowningly as her recent experiences of cruelty at Sarai's hands rose vividly in her memory.

His next words jolted her into amazement, for he began to speak of what would come, not of what was past. It seemed that what she had gone through was not a reason to leave, but what was going to happen was a reason to go back. 'You are going to have a child,' he said, looking down at her rounded belly, 'and it will be a son. From him will come numerous descendants. His name will be Ishmael, which means 'God hears', because God has heard you crying out in your desperation.'

He sat down beside her, leaning against the rock, and smiled with amusement as she continued to gape at him in open-mouthed astonishment. 'Oh yes,' he went on. 'God sees and hears you, you know. Now let me tell you about your son Ishmael.' He shook his head and laughed. 'He will be a tough one! In fact he'll be like a wild donkey, obstinate and strong. He will fight anyone who crosses him and I'm afraid he will not get on well with his brothers!' He pulled himself to his feet, and bent to pick up his bag and staff. 'Now, Hagar,' he said. 'You are actually quite close to the road you were looking for. The road to Shur is just over there.' He pointed with his staff. 'Fill your water skin and keep to the road.'

She was still staring at him, and now she too scrambled to her feet. He seemed to be on the point of leaving, and she called wildly, 'Where are you going?'

'Back,' he answered. And went. Suddenly he was not there anymore. 'The angel of the Lord,' she whispered to herself. 'I have seen the Lord, and he sees me!'

It was a wonderful sustaining thought and it strengthened her on the long walk back. It sustained her as she re-entered Abram's camp at Mamre and encountered the curious stares of the other servants. Even when Sarai spoke harshly to her, she remembered that God was watching her in her difficulties and was comforted. All the while she was in labour to bring forth her son, she was strengthened by that same knowledge, and she and Abram gave him the name 'Ishmael' as the angel of the Lord had said.

*   *   *

The fact that God is constantly seeing us should affect the way we live. For Hagar it was a revelation that God should even be aware of her – and further that he should care – but even more that he should come to her where she was in her distress. This is a pattern we see repeated through the Bible. God sees his people and is not indifferent to their cries. Some 400 years later the Israelites would be toiling in slavery under the merciless Egyptian sun. God had already chosen their deliverer, Moses. He spoke to him, also in a desert as it happens, and said, 'I have seen their distress and heard their cries,' and revealed his plan to Moses to rescue them.

Then in the New Testament, Jesus' disciples were in a boat on the Lake of Galilee in the middle of the night when a storm arose. It was life-threatening and they were terrified. But Jesus saw them and came to them where they were. The fact that Jesus sees us in our circumstances is something that we should remind ourselves of, as it is the antidote to the enemy's insidious whispers, 'He neither knows nor cares,' or, 'He has forgotten all about you.' In fact we are the apple of his eye! David knew this and pleaded, 'Keep me as the apple of your eye' (Psalm 17:8).

Another aspect of this comforted David: it was the knowledge that God also saw that the wicked abused the righteous. As he meditated on this, his frustration and desire for vengeance drained away (Psalm 94). The psalm begins with him calling on God to rise up and vindicate him. Then he thinks about how God is fully aware of what is going on; that it is the wicked who are ignorant; 'You fools, when will you become wise? . . . Does he who formed the eye not see?' (vv. 8–9). Not only is the Lord watching, he even knows the thoughts of men (v. 11). Now David's thoughts become positive and hopeful again: 'The Lord will not reject his people' (v. 14). By the end of the psalm he is back in a place of joy and security. 'The Lord has become my fortress' (v. 22).

This episode in the life of Abraham, Sarah and Hagar may seem strange to us and yet is so true to life. It shows that in God's economy the end does not justify the means. God had promised a son to Abraham, but resorting to manipulation of circumstances and ungodly methods to achieve that end simply introduced unlooked-for complications and confusion. But it is also reassuring to note that, however unrighteously the principal characters had behaved, God did not abandon his plan. He also continued to watch over Hagar, who carried Abraham's seed, and took her back to Abraham's dwelling place. It must have been hard for her to retrace her steps, to return to the scene of former humiliation and submit, but she obeyed, fortified by the knowledge that the God who had led Abraham and Sarah was watching over her too.

10

A New Name

Ishmael came storming in like a whirlwind, swinging his sling in one hand and a couple of dead conies (small rabbit-like creatures) in the other. He ran up to Abram excitedly, nearly tripping over a tent peg on the way.

'See what I've brought you, Father!' he yelled. Abram took the conies and laid them down on the grass beside him. 'Well done, son,' he said, ruffling the boy's long dark hair affectionately. 'Come and tell me how you got them!'

Ishmael squatted down by his father's chair and eagerly poured out the story of the hunt. Hagar watched from the shadows of the tent behind, noting the strong, sturdy limbs of the boy, his brown hands gesturing wildly as he described how he whirled the sling at his victims, his dark eyes flashing. Yes, he was becoming a wild donkey of a man. He was never still, always restless, active, tempestuous. He was a hard one to keep in check!

Abram's eyes rested on him with tenderness. The boy was strong and handsome, a hunter in the making. The old man loved him, loved his youth and vitality. Yet he was wild and unpredictable, untamed like a young colt that has not yet been broken in. He laughed with him now, enjoying the enthusiasm and drama of the boy's account.

A small child wandered up, the son of one of Abram's shepherds. Curiously he poked one of the dead conies, fingering and stroking its matted fur. Suddenly, Ishmael saw him and lashed out in fury. 'Leave it alone!' he shouted, and roughly pushed the child away. 'That's mine! Go away!' The little boy ran off, and Ishmael made as if to chase him, but Abram stood and caught hold of his hand. 'Ishmael! Son!' he remonstrated. He grasped his shoulders and turned the boy round to face him. 'There is no need to act so harshly,' he said quietly. 'Why are you so angry?'

The boy looked up at him from under lowered lashes, his face suddenly sullen and rebellious. As Abram looked into that face he saw there a mixture, a reflection of so much that was himself, but also the dark flashing eyes and full curved mouth and swarthy complexion so reminiscent of his mother, Hagar. He could feel the quivering movement of the boy's shoulders under his hands, squirming, impatient of the gentle restraint. He let him go, and he raced off, checked suddenly and ran back to pick up his sling from the ground where he had left it.

'There's a fox's den up there on the hill.' The words floated back to Abram from the energetic figure already pounding away across the field. He shook his head. 'A wild donkey of a man!' he said to himself, conscious again of feelings of disquiet. And yet he loved him, for was he not his own flesh and blood? It was one thing to father a son, he reflected, but quite another to raise him!

Sarai had also watched the scenario, and unhappiness stirred in her heart. She had watched Ishmael grow up these 13 years. She remembered the day he was born, the poignant cry of the new-born and how it had pierced her heart. For this was Abram's son! She could not help but love him. Her heart went out to him. She loved to hold his soft round baby form. But it was Hagar's breast that nourished him. It was

Hagar who sang to him softly as she fed him in the night hours, and it was Hagar whom he learned to call 'Mother'. Eagerly Sarai had looked for signs that were inherited from his father. 'Look, he has long fingers, just like his father!' she would say, or 'He has his father's nose!' Hagar would give her a sidelong glance, and passively agree. But anyone could see that his wide mouth, dark eyes and vigorous jet black curls proclaimed his Egyptian mother's heritage. Sarai was sure that he would grow tall and stately like Abram, but as he grew into adolescence, he remained short and stocky, muscular, with the powerful, sinewy arms and legs of a man who would rove the desert and be skilled with the bow and sling.

Her dreams of a child who would respond to loving affection soon died. He was not a cuddly baby! Even as an infant he was restless and energetic, impatient of hugs and kisses, and given to tantrums. Yet for Abram's sake she sought to love him, although he did little to return her affection. An uneasy truce had been established between her and Hagar ever since the maid had run away and then reappeared one day, exhausted and subdued. It was Abram who had questioned her about her wanderings, and it was he who had named the boy Ishmael. But Sarai had felt ashamed of her outburst of anger and had tried to be gentler towards her maid.

Now 13 years had passed, and Sarai had had plenty of time to reflect. Sometimes she thought back over the decades to the years in Ur. Did she regret the choice she and Abram had made? They had been cut out of a civilisation like stones hewn out of a quarry, but what had they been built into? Or were they destined simply to roll around Canaan like two displaced pebbles? There was no point in looking back. They had left the old life and they still carried a dream in their hearts of a new people and a new city. Their whole lives were given to pursuing the vision, even though they may never understand it or see it.

Sarai was content now to accept that motherhood was not for her. Ishmael was Abram's heir, and although he was a difficult boy there was nothing she could do about it. She drew closer to Abram in those years; her respect for him grew and deepened, and she was somewhat awed that he seemed to have a special relationship with the one he called El Adonai. He even went so far as to confide in her that he was the 'friend of God'.

Then everything changed again.

There was another night when the vast black sky was strewn with a myriad of stars and the man on the hilltop was again flung on his face, speechless in the great silence. Yet the silence was not empty. It was full and heavy with the awesome presence of his friend who had come to him before. This time he revealed himself by a new name, El Shaddai.[1] Then he reinforced his promise that Abram would become the father of a multitude: 'No longer shall your name be Abram[2] but Abraham.[3] I will make you exceedingly fruitful, and nations shall come from you, and kings shall come forth from you. And I will give to you and your descendants all the land of Canaan as an everlasting possession, and I will be their God.'

For a long time Abraham lay there endeavouring to take this all in. He had heard these promises before, yet each time they seemed to open out, become more detailed. Why was El Shaddai repeating these things? Had not Ishmael been born? He waited.

---

[1] The Lord Almighty. The root could also indicate 'Lord of the breasts', which came to be understood as the God of the mountains. Or possibly, the Lord of the Steppes, the great plains.

[2] Exalted Father.

[3] Father of a Multitude.

The voice spoke again: 'This will be the sign of the covenant between you and me; you shall circumcise every male in your household.'

Abraham got up from the cold ground and walked about to restore his circulation. He rubbed his cold hands together and thought about this new command. Circumcision was not unknown; in fact it was quite widely practised among Egyptians and other tribes around Canaan. But now El Shaddai was communicating that it was to be a special sign between them of the covenant they were in.

He stopped in his tracks. The voice was speaking again. He listened intently. It was about Sarai his wife! 'She shall no longer be Sarai, but Sarah.'[4] That was nice! There was to be honour and recognition for her as well! But wait . . . more was coming. 'I will bless her, and will surely give you a son by her. I will bless her so that she will be the mother of nations.'

Abraham was face down again, shaking, but this time with hysterical laughter. 'I am nearly a hundred,' he spluttered. 'Sarah will soon be ninety!' Although El Shaddai's presence was awesome, Abraham did not feel he was offended by his laughter. In fact he felt the divine presence was smiling too. After a while he sobered up enough to wipe his eyes on his sleeve and bring up the subject of Ishmael. 'If only Ishmael might inherit your promises,' he ventured. But the divine mind would not be deterred from his expressed intention. He repeated it now: 'Your wife Sarah will bear you a son and you will call him Isaac. I will establish my covenant with him.'

But what of Ishmael? 'I will bless Ishmael and will make him fruitful. He will be the father of twelve rulers and I will make of him a great nation.' Then he reverted to Sarah and

---

[4] Sarah literally means 'princess'.

the promised son: 'I will establish my covenant with Isaac, whom Sarah will bear this time next year.' This was breathtakingly clear and explicit. Never before had Abraham been given the name and the time of birth of the child.

God's presence lifted as the pale light of dawn began to light up the Eastern sky. Abraham made his way back thoughtfully to the tent. Sarah saw him stumble in and fall into bed, tired and chilled to the bone. Wisely she said nothing, but pulled a rug more securely around his shoulders and let him sleep. He would tell her in his own time!

She propped herself up on one elbow and gazed at his unconscious face, this old man of hers, so complex, so wanting to be righteous, so loving God, so striving to be obedient and yet so prone to human frailty! Yet he was God's friend. She had no doubt at all that he had been out communing with him alone in the night hours. Sometimes she regretted that she did not have the same direct close relationship with God. God did not talk to her in the same way. But then again, if God was talking to her husband, he was talking to her at the same time, for were they not one? She was glad that her husband had consistently believed in El Adonai ever since the first call from Ur, and, looking back, she could say that he had never failed them, although there were lots of things she did not understand.

She leaned over and gently kissed Abraham's lined face, and lay down beside him. She soon fell asleep again, as yet unaware that she was now renamed Princess, and he Father of Multitudes.

When she awoke much later, Abraham was searching for something in the tent. 'What are you looking for?' she asked sleepily.

'My flint knife,' was the unexpected reply. 'I thought I had put it in this chest.' He rummaged around.

'Why do you want it?' she yawned. He came back to the

bed and sat down by her. Then he lay down, his face close to hers on the pillow. He looked deep into her eyes and wondered how much of last night's revelation to tell her. She had been so much more contented lately, and he did not want to bring up those promises again of her bearing a son – not just now anyway. She would get upset all over again. Besides, the news of the circumcision was enough to cope with. Oh, and her new name! So he told her about that. They discussed it for a while, then he left her and went to gather all the males of his household and organise the ritual.

She grimaced to herself, and acknowledged that this was one of those occasions in life when she was profoundly grateful to be a woman. She was also gratified to learn that she was the recipient of a change of name. 'Sarah.' She tried it over a few times. True, it was not *much* different, but it did denote more honour than the old version. In fact the more she thought about it, the more happy she became. 'Just think,' she said to herself. 'That is how he thinks of me! I am old and barren; I have made some big mistakes. But he calls me his princess. I am honoured and loved.' And she was not talking about her husband now, but the faithful God who sees. She lay in her tent a long time, savouring the sweet revelation.

*   *   *

Names are often important in the Bible. They denoted some truth or revelation that the parent had received, or demonstrated some desire or vision for the child. Sometimes they were more like a nickname. For example 'Moses' has its roots in a verb meaning 'to draw out', because he was drawn out of the River Nile. 'Joshua' means 'deliverer', 'Joab' means 'Yahweh is father', 'Hannah' means 'gracious'. There were also occasions when God himself gave instructions for naming a child, as with Ishmael, Isaac, John (the Baptist)

and Jesus. Also there were times when God decided to give
a new name, and this was important because it signified that
the person had entered into a new revelation of God or come
into a new phase of relationship with him. Thus 'Jacob' ('the
supplanter') was renamed 'Israel' ('Prince with God' or 'one
who prevails').

A beautiful passage in Isaiah (62:2–4) speaks of the Lord
giving a new name to his people as a declaration that they
would leave behind a time of barrenness and enter into fruitfulness and fulfilment. He would own them and love them
like a tender bridegroom. 'You will be called by a new name
that the mouth of the Lord will bestow . . . No longer will
they call you Deserted, or name your land Desolate. But you
will be called Hephzibah [meaning "My delight is in her"]
and your land Beulah [meaning "married"].' So here, Sarah's
new name is a sign that she was leaving behind one phase in
her life and entering a new one. Perhaps up to now she had
not thought of herself as having any particular significance
to God, but from now on she was to walk with a new sense
of dignity and honour and unearned favour, because he
delighted in her!

Is there a hint here of another woman who was also called
to be the mother of one who would be the firstborn of a new
nation? Centuries later, an angelic messenger would speak to
an ordinary young woman in an obscure village and greet
her as 'highly favoured'. Since then, when God speaks to any
woman of his intention to put his life in her, she knows she
is chosen and favoured through no merit of her own. No
longer desolate or forsaken, she is to be a bearer of the life
of Jesus. What an honour! Her name is then inscribed in his
book: a permanent record of her place in his family.

No doubt there were a lot of sore, uncomfortable men and
boys around for the next few days. With characteristic obedience and thoroughness, Abraham made sure that all the

males in his household, Ishmael included, had their fore-skins removed. 'It will be a sign of the covenant between me and you,' God had said. A sign in what way? And to whom? Is not a sign to be seen? But this one would be concealed under clothing, so who was it for? And what did it denote?

Such an intimate sign surely must have been meant as a reminder to each individual that he was in a specific relationship with God. It was between him and his Maker; a reminder in his most private moments as to whom he belonged.

Then, secondly, it was literally a cutting off, a separation. It was a symbol in the flesh of a spiritual truth: that Abraham's children were to be a separate race, cut off, withdrawn from the carnal life of the rest of stricken humanity.

Thirdly, they were to see themselves as not only cut off *from*, but separated *into* the new family. It was to be not only a mark of exclusion, but also a mark of inclusion – a statement of belonging, with all its inherent benefits.

The apostle Paul expanded on this theme in the New Testament. The rite of circumcision had been observed all through the history of the Israelites. It had lapsed at times such as during the wanderings in the wilderness, but as they were preparing to enter the promised land God had commanded Joshua to reinstate it. They were to enter the land as a recognisable people, with a sense of belonging to God and to one another. They were not just a bunch of individuals straggling in but a people who bore in their bodies the mark of their common identity.

However, it eventually became an empty meaningless mechanical thing as the people forgot its significance. They forgot that God wanted first of all relationship, not cold ritual. Then Jesus came on the scene, to seek and save the lost and extend the offer of life to all humankind, not only the Jews.

Does this mean that all the foregoing history was now

obsolete? By no means, Paul argues! For all the history of
Israel pointed forward to this One who was to come and to
his people. We who believe in Jesus are now the family of
God and the children of Abraham.

Then what of circumcision? This became a big issue in the
early church; new Jewish believers could not quite bring
themselves to turn their backs on a whole culture that had
been kept so meticulously. For they believed that the keeping
of the Law with all its practices including circumcision
would achieve righteousness for them. Now Jesus the
paschal lamb had been slain, the sacrifice was made once for
all! Good news, but difficult to absorb in its entirety. Paul's
footsteps were constantly dogged by those coming behind
him, to undermine the freedom of the new converts, with
their insistence that their salvation was invalid unless they
submitted to circumcision.

In fact a sharp dispute arose in Antioch when some men
came and taught, 'Unless you are circumcised . . . you cannot
be saved'.[6] The issue had to be settled and the elders and
apostles met to discuss it. Peter eventually clinched it when
he stood and declared, 'God, who knows the heart, showed
that he accepted [the Gentiles] by giving the Holy Spirit to
them, just as he did to us. He made no distinction between
us and them for he purified their hearts by faith . . . it is
through the grace of our Lord Jesus Christ that we are
saved!' Bravo Peter! But it continued to be an ongoing con-
tention; some commentators suggest that these legalistic
Judaisers were the thorn in Paul's flesh of which he grew so
weary. Paul argues robustly in his letter to the Romans to the
effect that in Christ neither circumcision nor uncircumcision
is of any value; only faith expressing itself through love.

The church had been in peril of becoming just a little

---

[6] Acts 15:1

enclave within Judaism. This is why Paul had to be so adamant in withstanding all those who wanted to retain this particular sign, and other practices. All that went before – the temple, the passover and priestly system, the ark of the covenant, circumcision – were but shadows prefiguring the reality that found expression in Jesus and in the new era of the Spirit.

So much of the story of Abraham and Isaac is symbolic of a greater reality. For us, looking back from the shelter of the New Covenant, we can thank God, along with Paul, that God wants us to enter into all the benefits of 'the new circumcision'; that is, a separation of the heart from the world into a deep and lasting relationship with God through Jesus. For the history of Israel pointed forward to the one who was to come, and to his people. We who believe in Jesus are now the family of God, and can call Abraham our ancestor.

So Christians now must consider themselves cut off from the world. This is not something visible to surrounding people, but it is known to the individual and to God. We are in a new covenant, and the sign of this is a changed life. But just as Abraham circumcised his whole household as a sign of inclusion in the covenant made between him and God, so we also are brought into the household or family of God, qualified to share with all the saints the inheritance of the kingdom of light (Colossians 1:12).

11

The Visitation

Abraham was dozing in the drowsy afternoon in the doorway of his tent. The flocks were lying in what shade they could find, and the shepherds and servants were mostly sleeping. The bare brown hills shimmered in the intense heat. From this high vantage point, one could see for miles: ridge upon stony ridge dotted with bushes and scraggy thorn trees. Nearer, the slopes usually green with pasture in the spring and rainy seasons, had been yellow and dry for weeks now. The distant view was hazy and all was still, save for the rustling branches of the great oak trees around which Abraham's household was encamped. The oaks were a landmark for travellers, for they stood tall and stately, green even in drought.

Sarah was inside asleep on her bed. Abraham preferred to be here in the doorway, where he could see out and enjoy any gentle breeze that might stir the hot air. His head, with his curling white beard, sank lower onto his chest and soon he too was asleep. How long he slept he did not know, but it could not have been very long, for the short afternoon shadows had not lengthened much when suddenly he was awake.

Three men were standing there! Startled, he shook his head and blinked a few times, wondering if he were still dreaming. They were still there. Where could they have come from? One could see travellers approaching on these barren heights long before they arrived, and usually a small cloud of dust also heralded their coming. But he had seen no movement on the stony ridges, no dust cloud. Still shaking his head, he sought to gather his scattered wits, and scrambled to his feet. He hurried over to where they were standing and bowed low, as was the custom.

'My lords, you are welcome!' he exclaimed. 'Please go no further. Do me the honour of turning aside into my home. Let water be brought that you might refresh yourselves and rest, and let me prepare some food for you!'

'We will. Let it be as you have said!' the men replied.

Abraham called servants to bring seats for his guests and settled them comfortably in the shade, out of the searing heat. Then he ran into the tent. Sarah was still asleep and was startled out of her slumber by her husband urgently shaking her. 'We have guests!' he informed her.

'Who . . .' she began to ask sleepily.

But before she could get the question out, Abraham said, 'Quickly, Sarah, go and get some flour, the best finely ground flour, and make some loaves. I am going to choose a calf.'

Sarah was thoroughly awake now. She threw off her crumpled robe and pulled a fresh one over her head. Then she washed her face and combed her hair, twisted it up into a knot and covered it becomingly. Then she went out of the back of the tent to the household store. Calling one of the servant girls to her, she began measuring out the flour. As they pummelled the dough, she reflected that these must be special visitors if Abraham was killing a fatted calf for them. It was not long before a servant came in with the carcass of a calf and set about preparing it. Soon the kitchen tent was full of bustle and stir as the oven was heated, herbs were chopped and curds were poured into dishes.

Sarah peeped out of the door to get a glimpse of these honoured guests, but they were seated with their backs to the kitchen and she could not see their faces. Abraham had set up a trestle table under the tree and was pouring wine and offering cheese while they waited for the main meal to be cooked. Sarah sent out platters of fruit, and soon fragrant mounds of fresh bread were also set on the table. Then, with his own hands, Abraham carried out the dish of tender calf and served it to them. The appetising aroma wafted tantalisingly on the still air, and Sarah watched anxiously to see how the meal was received. Evidently it was satisfactory, for they ate heartily.

She was preparing to retreat into the kitchen tent to start clearing the debris, when she was arrested by the sound of her own name. 'Where is Sarah, your wife?' one of the men asked. She stopped in her track, one hand on the door post.

'She is in the tent,' replied Abraham. She wondered if he were going to call her over and introduce her, so she hovered, waiting. What happened next was totally unexpected. The man who had spoken said calmly to Abraham, 'I am going to come this way again next year. By then, Sarah will have a son of her own.'

Sarah gasped, and then catching sight of her aging husband standing before his guests, bent and stooping with his curly white beard blowing in little wisps around him, she giggled. Then seeing her own veined and wrinkled hand on the doorpost, the fingers crooked and knobbly, the giggle became a bubble of hysterical laughter that threatened to engulf her. She clapped the old woman's hand over her mouth and backed into the tent. 'How crazy!' she wanted to shout. 'He can't know how old I am, or Abraham! I have been past child bearing for years! And not only that . . . how can Abraham and I even contemplate intercourse after all this time? That pleasure belongs in the distant past!'

Shoulders shaking, she collapsed onto a chair inside the doorway. As she sank onto the chair, her hands passed down over her breasts, limp and pendulous with age, and she laughed again, but there was pain mixed in the mirth, for why reopen that distressing subject? That door had been firmly sealed for many years against further disappointment! It seemed unfair to force it open; to make her confront once more that land of lost hopes and dreams, which she had so successfully put behind her. 'Don't unsettle me now!' she wanted to whimper. 'I have learned to live with it. I have no more expectations in that direction. The wound has closed, the scar has healed. Don't open it up! Don't make me think about it any more! I don't want to go there again.'

Through the open doorway, a clear resounding voice reached her. 'Why did Sarah laugh?' As suddenly as the laughter had come upon her, now fear sobered her. She was amazed, for she had not thought her reaction had been audible. She had not wanted to be rude to their guests and had endeavoured to smother her laughter, but something in his voice filled her with a trembling awe. 'Why did Sarah laugh? Why did she say, "Shall I indeed bear a son when I am so old?"'

She got up from her seat and walked hesitantly out of the tent. As she shuffled towards the speaker he turned round and spoke to her. She knew his eyes were boring into her, but she could not lift her head. 'Is anything too difficult for the Lord?' he asked gently. Dumbly she looked up then into a strong enigmatic face, shadowed by the head-dress commonly worn by men, and encountered a look of tender compassion and understanding. 'I shall come again next year and by then you will have a son,' he repeated.

Her heart racing, she tried to cover for her reaction. 'I did not laugh,' she faltered, for she was afraid of those penetrating eyes. She was beginning to wonder if this guest was the one whom Abraham had spoken to before on several occasions, in the night.

Again that firm but gentle voice: 'No. You did laugh, Sarah.' He would not be contradicted. Clarity; knowledge, intimate awareness of the turmoil of emotions within her: I know you better than you know yourself, Sarah. I know your age, your pain, your dead hopes. I also know the plans I have for you, the same ones that I always had.

The men rose from the table and walked over to a place where they could overlook the plain. Sodom was just visible in the distance. Abraham joined them.

But Sarah crept, trembling, into her own tent. She lay down on her bed, bemused, almost breathless. Those words hung like shining jewels against the swirling dark confusion of her mind. She whispered them to herself again and again: 'Is anything too difficult for the Lord?' The weight of her thoughts pressed her down upon the bed. Could it be possible that she had spoken with God? Adonai? Elohim? El Shaddai? Who else could know her thoughts, her disappointments, her sadness? Who else would dare to speak of them and make predictions with such calm authority? She lay there hardly daring to move, the awesome glimmering of understanding robbing her of strength.

'Is anything too difficult for the Lord?' She tried it another way: 'Is anything too wonderful? Or too miraculous for him to do?'

She knew they were God's words, and the more she contemplated them the more persuaded she became, because something was happening to her. A tiny germ of hope was stirring like a living thing in her heart. Her thoughts centred increasingly on the one who had said them. She felt weak with the wonder of it. The Lord! Was it really the Lord? Now she began to understand how Abraham had felt when God had spoken to him; she understood why he had seemed sometimes so amazed, so overwhelmed and yet so certain of what he had heard, and why it caused him to change the direction of his life. She knew that Abraham no longer worshipped the moon because he had had dealings with the one who made the moon. She knew that he had had encounters with this wonderful yet terrifying being and that he regarded himself as the friend of God. She had accepted that; she had gone along with it. But now for the first time she herself was confronted by his word and his person.

As she continued to lie there on her bed she was gripped with a sort of fear. And yet was it fear? More a wonder, even a joy, began to rise in her, and yet there was a fear. The wonder was that this God who had always spoken to Abraham before, had now come to *her.* He had singled her out, come to her, revealed himself to her. But the fear was that she had laughed in scorn; she had disbelieved him, dismissed his word. Now she turned over on the bed and, burying her face, put her hands over her head. How could she have done that? Now what would he do to her?

Then she remembered those words again. He knew she had laughed, but he had not acted in anger. What had he done? He had repeated the promise; he had said again those preposterous words about her having a son. She turned over again and sat up, and contemplated her body. She looked at her hands and feet, arms and legs. She could see all too plainly how they had lost their muscle tone, how the skin was wrinkly. She patted her abdomen and her breasts. Everything was floppy and fallen. She thought about her womb, now dry and unfunctional. Something like despair began to come on her again. 'I can't! I can't!' she whispered to herself. And what about her husband? 'He can't either! Neither of us can!'

She lay back upon the pillow. How strange that a few minutes ago she was full of wonder, almost excitement, but

now simply felt old and tired and hopeless again. She wished
she could stay in the happy mood. She had felt so good when
she was thinking about those words and the one who had
said them. Dreamily she recalled the whole incident, from
the moment Abraham had shaken her awake to the moment
the guest had spoken her name. She relived hearing him
speak that she would have a baby, her laughter, her shame at
the disclosure of it, and then that question: 'Is anything too
miraculous for the Lord?' Once again the sense of awe came
upon her.

Slowly she got up from the bed and went to the door of the
tent. It was totally dark now. Vaguely she wondered where
Abraham was, little knowing that at that moment he was
having an extraordinary conversation with the Lord about
the future of the town of Sodom. There was some chatter
issuing from the direction of the cooking tent as the servants
were finishing their work, and she could hear the sound of a
sheep coughing in the distance. A dog barked and there were
a few restless movements from some donkeys nearby.
Gradually everything quietened down and all was still.

She had seen the sky at night many times before, but
somehow tonight it was particularly spectacular. She pulled
her shawl around her tightly and walked a little way beyond
the cluster of tents to a ridge, and stood gazing at the millions of blazing stars. She felt very small, and the sky seemed
very large.

'Is anything too hard for the Lord?' The words came again
with an urgent intensity. Too hard for the one who created
all these stars? Too difficult for *him*? Ludicrous thought! He
was huge, immense, beyond understanding, thought or
reason. With one flick of the wrist he had splattered hand-
fuls of stars across the face of the universe. He was *big*!

If it was a serious question the answer had to be, 'No, NO,
NO! Nothing was too hard for the Lord.' Objectively that

was true. That little germ of hope was stirring again. But what about that particular issue of her giving birth to a son? She could believe God could do anything, but could she believe specifically for *this*?

She almost fell into despondency again as she began to think about her own limitations. After a while she realised that when she thought about herself, hope drained away. But when she thought about God and his greatness, hope would rise. But was hope enough?

The deep certainty that *he* had spoken to *her* began to change hope into faith. It was not only that he had said those words, but that he had said them to her. It was his idea, his initiative, his expressed will. It was not her trying to wring something out of a reluctant God; it was, if anything, the other way round: *he* was having to convince *her*.

Something was exploding in her heart. Excitement was bubbling up – a joy, an anticipation of what God was going to do. It was not about her any more: her limitations, her feebleness, her failure. It was all about his power, his plans and his calm assurance that it would happen. She was entering into faith. Now there was a deep and serene inner knowing that what he had spoken would come to pass.

She threw off her shawl and whirled it around her head, laughing, but this time with joy. 'No!' she cried. 'Nothing is too hard or wonderful or difficult for you! Nothing! Even me and Abraham having a baby is not too miraculous for you. You are the God of wonders.' She flung out her arms and danced around like a young woman, faith growing with every step and spin, feeding on the words he had spoken: 'Is anything too hard for the Lord?' Her gyrations came to a stop, and she sat down abruptly on the stony ground. She thought again of those eyes looking at her. They seemed now to be smiling.

She went back to the tent, walking tall with the assurance

of a woman who knows she has been with God. Something had happened to her today. She was not the same woman who had fallen asleep in the afternoon. Now there was a deep knowing that God valued her personally; that he did not only regard Abraham; that he had disclosed truth to her that changed her whole perspective about herself, her life and her God.

In the days that followed she continued to meditate on what God had said, and to thank him for what he was going to do. She came to a place of rest and peace in her spirit, although she did not yet see the outcome of the promise. But in her heart it was as good as done.

*   *   *

Without faith it is impossible to please God. Hebrews 11 is a chapter full of God's heroes, who are examples to us in faith. 'By faith even Sarah herself received ability to conceive even beyond the proper time of life, since she considered Him faithful who had promised' (v. 11, NASB). It is God's word that produces faith. God's specific word to Sarah lifted her beyond her physical and emotional limitations into a realm where the supernatural could happen.

But faith is not a passive, static thing. It must be acted upon if it is to be productive. It was one thing to believe that God *could* do it, and then to believe he *would* do it, but unless she and Abraham got together and went into action, nothing would happen!

*   *   *

Abraham still had not come back when Sarah awoke next morning. She lay for a while in a happy stupor, remembering yesterday's remarkable events, and then fell to thinking about her husband and how she was going to communicate to him what had happened to her.

'Shall we indeed have pleasure?' she thought. She was glad that her reminiscences of their union in the past could be described as 'pleasure'. It was a long time now since they had enjoyed intercourse. Abraham had fathered Ishmael at the ripe age of 86. That was 13 years ago, and she could not remember if she and Abraham had ever made love after that. She was inclined to think after he had slept with Hagar, that had signalled the end of that particular marital activity. But she knew that if they were to start again now, Abraham would need a miracle as well as her. However, she knew also that her husband was a man of faith, and they both believed in a faithful God; she suspected that it would not be difficult to persuade Abraham that they could again have 'pleasure'!

Later in the morning, as she was going about the business of the day, there was a sudden dull booming sound and the ground seemed to shudder and vibrate. She became aware of a strange darkness stealing over the land, and a smoky sulphurous smell in the air. It seemed to come from the plain over to the east, where the city of Sodom was located. The servants stopped their work and looked around apprehensively, and then they all began to move to a high ridge where they could see out over the plain. Horrified, they stood watching as a vast plume of smoke arose from the direction of Sodom. The very earth seemed to have opened up; fire gushed out and cinders and debris rained down. The air was thick with choking fumes as the wind blew the smoke westward. Soon they could not see clearly and, coughing and spluttering and holding hands to running eyes and noses, they ran back and took refuge in tents and anywhere they could find.

Sarah was searching for Abraham, and suddenly saw his figure looming out of the grey, ashy gloom. She ran to him and pulled him back into their tent. Tears were streaking down the dust on his face. 'Lot! What has happened to Lot?' she asked urgently.

He made a gesture of hopelessness. 'I don't know,' he sighed. 'Sodom must be destroyed by now. I don't know if Lot and his family were able to escape.'

Sarah was silent as she thought of Lot's pretty, foolish wife and their attractive daughters.

Then Abraham sat down and recounted to her how he had spent yesterday evening pleading for the city of Sodom to be saved from the judgement of God. After their guests had eaten, she remembered seeing them walk over to the ridge with Abraham. Then she had crept shaking into the tent. Now she found out that as they looked down over the plain they had talked together. One of them had said that the depravity of Sodom had reached such a pitch that he could tolerate it no more. Then two of them had turned away and gone down towards Sodom. Abraham was left standing before the third, the one who had spoken.

'It was the Lord, Sarah,' he said quietly. Again she was seized by trembling awe and simply nodded. Then, as if amazed by his own audacity, Abraham related how he had asked if God would sweep away the righteous with the wicked. God had assured him that if he found 50 righteous he would spare the city. Abraham knew that it was unlikely there would be so many, so he pleaded for 45, then 40, then 30, then 20, until eventually he had God's promise that if he found only ten righteous people he would spare the entire city.

Abraham stopped speaking for a while. Then he took Sarah's hand and with tears in his eyes whispered, 'He was so willing to give mercy! He will not let such wickedness continue unchecked, but for the sake of a few he would save the many. He is a gracious God, Sarah: slow to anger and abounding in mercy. But the sin of Sodom must have been great indeed that he should destroy it.' Still Sarah said nothing. Abraham said slowly, 'I wonder if he would have spared the city if I had gone on pleading.' He looked at her now, his eyes full of sadness.

'We shall never know,' she said.

'No,' he replied, 'but we do know that he who is the judge of all the earth will only do what is right.'

The destruction of the city had a sobering effect on them all, and for a few days everyone was in a state of shock and fear at the violence of the earthquake or volcanic eruption. Abraham and Sarah went together and stood looking out at the scene of devastation. The vegetation was no more and the landscape was entirely rearranged. Once Sodom had stood on the shores of the Salt Sea, but now the lake had become enlarged and covered the whole stricken area, and Sodom had vanished. The menacing steely grey waters lay between barren desolate hills and already salt was encrusting its still-smoking shores.

Later they heard that the two men who had gone down to Sodom had been angels. They had pleaded with Lot and his family to leave with all haste. But they had been reluctant, blind to the immense danger they were in. At last, the angels seized them by the hand and almost forced them to flee, urging them not to look back or linger lest they be overtaken by disaster. Lot and his daughters ran, but his wife dawdled and lingered. The last they saw of her was her still figure covered in ash and dust as it rained down out of the sky.

Sarah's understanding of God was filling out all the time. Both his power in creation and his power to destroy displayed his might. He could do all that, yet he was still willing to be entreated by one puny man for mercy. He was awesomely great, but ready to converse as a friend with one individual. Looking out across that devastated landscape, their instinct was to bow before this terrifying but compassionate God, and worship.

It took a while for the dust in the atmosphere to settle, and for a few weeks the stars were indistinct and less visible. But one night in the early autumn, as the air grew colder, they blazed with their former brilliance. Abraham looked up and said to Sarah, 'See those stars? God promised me that our descendants would be as numerous as those!'

'Yes!' she replied without hesitation. 'I believe it!'

Abraham turned to her with a delighted smile. 'Do you really?' he exclaimed. 'What has happened to you?'

A little shyly she told him of how the word from God had produced faith in her heart. 'You know that I am well past child bearing now; my womb is as good as dead. But I believe that God who made the promise is faithful,' she finished.

Abraham was moved. He was not unmindful of all her struggles over the years. She had stood by him, followed him out of Ur, then Haran. Then there had been that uncomfortable episode in Egypt, and the whole debacle with Hagar. Sarah had been so attractive and vibrant, and he had seen her sorrow as the inevitable aging process had taken its course, until all hope of bearing children had ceased. Now as she told him of the fresh upspringing of faith in her heart, he felt closer to her than he had for many years, and his love for her surged up again.

'Sarah, you know that I too am as good as dead as far as having children is concerned,' he said. 'But for a long time now I have believed in God and in his power to keep his promises. I have enjoyed friendship with him and think I have found favour with him.' He said this humbly, without any arrogance; he simply knew that faith was pleasing to God. 'But my faith is not enough on its own. This has to be something that we do together.'

Sarah smiled in the darkness, and squeezed his hand. She wanted to say, 'Let's give it a try!' but instead she said demurely, 'I'll be waiting in the tent.' After a little while, he followed her. As he parted the curtains that hung by the bed, he thought she had never been more desirable, and he felt like a young man again. He reached out to her and her last coherent thought was, 'God is giving us pleasure again!'

Thus Abraham and Sarah became the father and mother of all those who live by faith – a nation as numerous as the stars or the sand on the seashore.

12

The Abimelech Episode

Unbelievably, Abraham did it again. He put Sarah in a position of embarrassment and compromise, even possible danger. It was odd really. They were living through perhaps the most important year of their lives; in fact one of the most significant years for humanity in terms of the development of salvation history. God had come to them both with his word, and they had received it and acted upon it in faith. Thereafter in the pages of Scripture both would be upheld as models of overcoming faith. Sarah may even have been pregnant with the miracle baby by then! Yet what happened next could have endangered him.

For some reason Abraham decided to leave the Oaks at Mamre and journey south, pitching his camp in the region of Gerar. Perhaps the pastures up at Mamre had grown sparse and thin, and were more lush on the lower plains.

In Gerar, Abimelech was the ruling man of influence and power. He soon heard that Abraham had arrived in his territory and sent messengers to find out more about him. They returned with the information that he was a wealthy man, travelling with a very comely woman whom he referred to as his sister. By all accounts she was an unusual woman – cultured, intelligent, elegant. 'Strange!' thought Abimelech.

'Why is such a woman wandering the desert? And unmarried?' Intrigued, he sent a message that he would like to meet her.

What were Abraham and Sarah's thoughts upon receiving this message? Surely their minds must have returned to the incident in Egypt some 25 years earlier. Perhaps they both thought that Sarah was not the woman she had been then; she had by now lost the bloom of her earlier beauty, being nearly 90. There was no likelihood that she would be appealing as a potential wife! Even so, Abraham still prevailed upon her to identify herself as his sister rather than his wife in order to protect himself.

We can imagine Sarah sighing and thinking 'Here we go again! He is more concerned about his own safety than mine!' But perhaps she also thought, 'I am a more secure and mature woman now than I was then. I can handle any difficulty that emerges.' It is unclear why they resorted to this half-truth, but it is evident that Abraham secured her collusion to it. It is also clear that Abimelech acted in all innocence and integrity, believing that Sarah was a free woman. He liked her and took her into his household intending to have her as a wife. Perhaps he had expectations of a large dowry from a rich man such as Abraham.

Abraham's actions appear to be the result of jumping to conclusions. He did not investigate to find out what sort of man Abimelech was, but simply assumed from the start that he was unscrupulous and ungodly. Later on he would say defensively, 'I was sure there was no fear of God in this place and they would kill me because of my wife.' As it happens he was wildly wrong: Abimelech was a man of unusual integrity, and feared God. Fortunately, Abimelech treated Sarah with respect and courtesy. He did not force himself upon her or molest her in any way.

One wonders how long this state of affairs would have

continued had Abimelech not had a very scary dream. Suddenly, God himself spoke to him as he slept and told him he was as good as dead because he had taken another man's wife! In terror, Abimelech protested that he had acted in all innocence. Both Abraham and Sarah had told him they were brother and sister, and he had acted with all integrity. God replied that he knew that and that was why he had kept him from touching her.

Then God said a very strange thing: he told Abimelech to restore Sarah to her husband and to ask Abraham to pray for him, 'for he is a prophet and will pray for you and you will live'. How extraordinary that God uttered not one word of censure about Abraham, but upheld him as a prophet, a man of spiritual authority! It was Abimelech who felt shame, being caught in a transgression, not Abraham – who had caused it!

In the morning, Abimelech called his servants together and told them about the dream. They were full of fear. Abimelech sent someone to bring Abraham back to his dwelling. When he arrived, Abimelech faced him in some anguish and cried, 'Why did you place me and my household in this jeopardy? What have I done to deserve this?'

Lamely Abraham replied, 'I thought that there was no fear of God in this place, and that you would kill me because of my wife. Besides, she is my step-sister.'[1] He then disclosed that they had agreed years ago when they took up the nomadic life to identify themselves as brother and sister as they travelled about.

---

[1] Some commentaries suggest that Sarah was not his half-sister (Genesis 20:12) i.e. the daughter of Terah, but not of the same mother as Abraham. Genesis 11:31 describes her as Terah's daughter-in-law, not his daughter. So perhaps she was an adopted daughter (see *The New International Commentary* on Genesis by Victor Hamilton, pp 380–384).

Far from being the unscrupulous person Abraham had expected, Abimelech continued to act with dignity and nobility. He not only quickly restored Sarah, but showered gifts on Abraham and insisted that he was free to come and go, and settle in any part of his land as he chose. He also gave him a gift of money and made it clear that there was no stigma attached to Sarah: her reputation was intact.

What a strange incident! Why would Abraham put his wife through this ordeal not once but twice? And why now when there was so much at stake? Had he not learned from the first time? Why was he so quick to assume the worst from a man he did not know? Many suggestions are offered by many scholars; none seems satisfactory. There may have been some cultural reasons that elude us today.

And how did Sarah feel about it? We can only guess, and infer certain things from other passages of Scripture.

We have seen that Abraham and Sarah were chosen by God to be the parents of a child who would be the first of a new nation. They were called out from the surrounding culture to follow God, and they were obedient. But we have also seen that they were far from perfect. First, Abraham took them into Egypt, where he nearly lost his way, his wife and his integrity. Then he yielded to his wife's manipulations to produce an heir by Hagar, which resulted in Sarah treating Hagar cruelly. Now they were resorting to devious half-truth again . . . all of which goes to show that they were by no means exemplary in every way!

However, they are upheld as examples in very specific areas. Sarah particularly is shown to be a role model in the New Testament for the way she related to her husband. Included in 1 Peter 3 is a section of teaching for wives and husbands in the early church. It exhorts wives to be submissive to their husbands and, rather than concentrating on their outward appearance, to cultivate an inner beauty consisting of a 'gentle and quiet spirit, which is of great worth in God's sight' (v. 4). It goes on to say that this is how the 'holy women of the past' behaved, 'like Sarah, who obeyed Abraham and called him her master' (vv. 5–6). Then comes the challenge: 'You are her daughters if you do what is right and do not give way to fear' (v. 6).

It seems that Sarah practised something that we would think of as a contradiction in terms; namely, submission without fear. Confident submission. Is there such a thing? Surely submission, by very definition, indicates a lack of confidence! Does it not mean that you put yourself under the authority of someone, resigning the right to make your own decisions, and generally acting as if inferior? Surely one can only submit if one is full of fear, unsure of one's abilities or strengths or rights. A person who is secure and confident, able and strong, does not submit.

Yet here we are told that Sarah submitted to her husband and did not give way to fear. Fear of what? Fear of what would happen if she did what her husband asked her to do, even if it was something she did not want to do? Fear that she could be abandoned in another man's household? Fear that all the sacrificial obedience of leaving Ur and its comforts was a waste of time? Fear that Abraham did not truly love her? Fear that just as she had come to a new place of faith, all would now be lost and ruined? This episode with Abimelech was an opportunity to test the quality of her submission. There had probably been many others before this, but this is one we know about (and of course the similar episode in Egypt with Pharaoh).

There were many fears that she could have given way to, but she did not allow those fears to overcome her. She went ahead and made herself vulnerable in obedience to Abraham. Are we suggesting then that what he wanted was right? No! He was acting in a despicably selfish and cowardly way. He was not acting as a godly covering and protection. In fact he was almost abdicating his responsibility towards her, by putting himself first.

Are we saying then that she went into this in a detached, mindless way, suspending her opinions and emotions? I don't think so. The passage in 1 Peter 3 seems to indicate that she had been cultivating an attitude of heart, so that her response when called on to submit to her husband was that of a 'gentle and quiet spirit', something she had been working on. She walked into the situation with her eyes open, with intelligence and trust.

Trust? Trust in whom? Trust in Abraham? Not entirely. She knew her husband. She had been with him for many decades, and knew all his many strengths, but also his weaknesses. I suggest she had faith in the principle of submission, because she had faith in the God who initiated it. Ultimately it was God in whom she trusted. She had proved his reliability before when she was in a similar situation; she could trust him now to keep her from harm.

She did not only obey Abraham when it suited her. Submission is meaningless if it is only carried out when it coincides with the will of the one required to submit. The very essence of Christian submission is that the will is brought into line with the one who makes the demands. Sarah practised a principle, and she did not believe that a bad experience negated the principle.

This is where Sarah can stand as a great example of faith to us. Christian submission is not simply a matter of pragmatism. No Christian principle is a matter of pragmatism. God's principles are God's ways, and God's ways are not our ways. They are contrary to human wisdom and philosophy. They have to be embraced by faith, and they have to be expressed and worked out by faith. Pragmatism says, 'OK, I'll give it a go and see if it works', and when it appears not to work, it gives up and says, 'I'll find another way that suits me better.' Faith says, 'God requires it and I trust him, so that settles it. If it goes against my natural inclinations, I must find his grace to do it.'

Many Christians give up at the first hurdle when confronted with a new challenge. For example, they hear a sermon on, say, prayer. They pray. They don't receive the answer they want, so they give up, saying, 'It doesn't work.' But faith says, 'I will still pray, because God tells me to.' They do not realise that it is not only getting the answer that is important: God is also working things into them along the way. Character is being formed, self is being crucified, and an obedient heart is being cultivated.

It is the same with Christian submission. It is not a matter of 'Does it work?' – in other words, 'What do I get out of it?' It is to do with believing that God is good and that what he wants is therefore good. So if he requires me to submit to my husband, then that must be good! I will trust him for the consequences.

Now there may be all sorts of things standing in the way, but they probably boil down to only two: my unwillingness, and my husband's weakness or over-authoritarianism. Basically I don't want to, and he isn't worthy of it! I can't trust him enough not to take advantage of my submission. Either I will be wiped out by his demands and end up as a doormat, or the home will fall apart because he is unable to take the lead. He is either too weak or too strong to be worthy of my submission.

I think that behind Sarah's submission to her husband was a much bigger thing: submission to God. When she obeyed Abraham she was in fact expressing her faith that God would look after her. Abraham asked his wife to do a totally unreasonable thing. She did not argue; she submitted without fear. What happened? God vindicated her faith. She not only came out of it unscathed; she came out considerably richer, with her reputation untarnished and Abimelech swearing undying allegiance to Abraham!

Submission to God is powerful. That is why the enemy has got hold of the idea and twisted it and lied to us that it is unreasonable, unworkable and utterly repellent. Humans hate it! Why? Because in the beginning the serpent whispered to Eve, 'You can be like God.' So that is what we run after – the lie that we can be our own gods, and do what we like whenever we like in whatever way we like. In fact, the essence of godlikeness, as we understand it, is to please ourselves.

Submission is the total antithesis: it is all about pleasing Jesus and serving others. It is about cultivating a servant heart. The devil not only hates that, he fears and dreads it. Jesus modelled it and it is powerful. It is the mark of another kingdom. When husbands and wives 'esteem one another highly in love'; when Christians wash one another's feet; when people deny themselves and take up their cross – the kingdom is coming in.

What about the rest of the advice in 1 Peter 3? The account in Genesis repeatedly tells us that Sarah was a beautiful woman. I wonder what she was like at 90? Evidently there was something about her even at that age that attracted Abimelech! Yet in 1 Peter it appears that Christian women must not be concerned with outward appearance. It is interesting that the Bible often takes the trouble to point out that a woman was beautiful; Rebekah, Rachel, Esther and Abigail, among others, are described in this way. Then of course the Song of Solomon is devoted to dialogue between two lovers, and there are frequent and detailed descriptions of their beauty.

Beauty is important to God. He made us and he wants women to be confident in their femininity; to enjoy it and be secure in it. Our bodies are the outward temple in which the spirit resides. The spirit will last for ever, but the body is a temporary residence, so it is short-sighted to put all our efforts into maintaining the temple.

The prevailing mood today is an obsession with appearance. Vast sums are spent on clothes and make-up, and fortunes are made and lost almost overnight in the fickle fashion world – where suddenly a young woman becomes the 'face' of today and is obsolete tomorrow; where a style is 'in' this season and 'out' the next; where designer labels become the defining factor of whether the wearer is acceptable or not – and all the time people are starving, children are being abused, exams have to be written, sick people must be cared for. In fact, values have become topsy turvy, where the trivial is seen as important and the urgent is neglected. Maybe the preoccupation with clothes is a sort of escapism, a retreat into frivolity from a world we are ill-equipped to deal with. In any case it is often the young who are the targets. They are the ones who are exploited by the fashion trade and become victims, agonising over their weight, their hair or their lack of designer gear.

Sarah was beautiful. The Bible is unequivocal about that. Let's not be afraid of beauty! But let's appreciate it without being obsessed by it. Some women feel bewildered and lost because someone was excited by their body and took their pleasure without thought of what they were doing to the emotions, self-image and sense of identity that are now shattered. These women now equate beauty with lust, sex and hatred. It is hard for them to accept and appreciate their beauty free from these associations. So they deny it and retreat into neglect, or maybe they over-compensate with orgies of clothes-buying, or try to bury the pain with lots of activity and distractions.

Only God can reconstruct the broken image and give

courage to find confidence again in one's femininity when it has been spoiled and besmurched. Also, only God can give back what has been robbed from us: the priceless gift of being able to look in the mirror and see someone there who is clean and secure.

Many have profound feelings of anxiety about their bodies because they have used them carelessly. They have slept around, or starved themselves, or over-indulged in food, or abused their bodies with drugs, drink or nicotine. When a person comes to the realisation that they need a saviour, God not only saves their soul, but begins to change their mind so that they start to see themselves differently. Their bodies are now the dwelling place of the Holy Spirit! In fact the apostle Paul calls them the Holy Spirit's 'temple'. When the Temple in Jerusalem had been corrupted by wrong use, Jesus came to clean it up and give it a new function as a house of prayer. Now we as individuals (as well as corporately) have this new designation: to be clean and holy and dedicated to his service.

Amazingly, millions who were once totally given to self-indulgence of every kind, exploited, used, broken, sick, warped and depraved, have now been washed and cleansed and have heard the voice of Jesus saying, 'You are altogether beautiful, my darling, and there is no blemish in you' (Song of Solomon 4:7, NASB).

Sarah's example from thousands of years ago is a good one. She was able to receive the fact that she was beautiful, but what she concentrated on was her 'inner beauty', a gentle and quiet spirit.

I used to read that passage with a wry smile, thinking, 'Well, that would be nice! Too bad I'm not very quiet or gentle!' Then one day I saw it in a different light. The verse actually says that a gentle and quiet spirit is precious to God. He likes it! Around that time, I went to India with my husband, and a couple of friends from our church came to look after the children. When I came back I asked my daughter how things had gone. 'Oh, Mum!' she exclaimed. 'We had such a lovely time! And I love being with Auntie Liz. She is so gentle.'

Now I was seriously thinking! The passage in 1 Peter 3 is not idly suggesting that if you have it, you have it, and if you don't, tough. It is actually encouraging us to cultivate these beautiful characteristics deliberately and saying that Sarah was a role model for us. As I thought and prayed about it, I saw that gentleness is a fruit of the Spirit. God is gentle, and he wants us to show this beautiful quality. A 'quiet spirit' does not necessarily mean that you never say anything! I believe you can be a vocal, energetic person but still have a quiet spirit. It is to do with the heart. It is about knowing serenity and security, which comes from a heart at rest in God, whatever the circumstances.

Sarah learned that.

13

Isaac Comes, Ishmael Goes

I was shopping in Missouri, USA, for my pregnant daughter and went into a store full of beautiful maternity outfits. The shop assistant was most helpful and showed great interest in my daughter Anna, who lives in South Africa. As we discussed the relative merits of different outfits – long and short, pinafores and trouser suits, T-shirts and casual wear – I wished heartily that such a shop had been available when I was pregnant many years ago. I remember wearing one second-hand dress during most of my first pregnancy and afterwards vowing that I would never wear the thing again!

The variety here was stunning and I was having difficulty making up my mind what to buy. I was also trying to visualise how big Anna was likely to get and was therefore uncertain what size to buy. The shop assistant came to my rescue with a helpful suggestion. 'Is your daughter normally a similar size to you?' she asked. 'Yes,' I replied.

'Well, why not try some things on? We have a little cushion you can tie round your waist with tapes to help you get the approximate size of a pregnancy at six months.'

I thought this was simply hilarious, and had an amusing time trying on garments and pretending to be pregnant again! I wished I had a friend with me to share the fun and perhaps take a misleading picture . . .

I am 54 years old and well past the capacity for child-bearing, but it got me thinking about what it must have been like for Sarah to become pregnant at the age of 90. I think I have tended to grossly under-estimate the extraordinary nature of this miracle. Imagine: even if she was in exception-ally good physical condition, with no osteoporosis resulting in stooping shoulders and bent spine, her muscle tone must have been slack. How could an aged uterus and abdomen support the weight of a foetus? And how could she find the enormous energy required to push it out into the world? What about breast-feeding? How could old and flabby breasts fill with milk? The more I think about it, I realise that this was not just a miracle of conception, but of sustaining the life of the baby through its development in the womb, of supplying supernatural strength to give birth to it, and of providing the necessary resources to feed it. Truly this woman grew strong in every way as she believed in God! The birth of Isaac was a breathtaking miracle. Those few words, 'Sarah became pregnant and bore a son', hide a multitude of detail.

*   *   *

Abraham was out tending his flocks when a servant came with the message that Sarah's labour had begun. He hurried over the fields. As he drew near the tent, he could hear her panting and groaning as the contractions mounted in inten-sity. It was a protracted labour as elderly muscles fought to cope with this new experience, but sometime around dawn, with a last rending effort, the baby was born.

Exhausted but radiant, the 90-year-old mother looked up at the 100-year-old father and smiled. Abraham took his son in his arms and, almost unable to speak for joy, he whispered, 'Isaac, my Isaac!' (Isaac means 'laughter'.)

'Yes,' said Sarah weakly, 'God has given me laughter after all these years of sorrow. Everyone who hears about this will laugh with me'.

Together they gazed at the child of promise in wonder and delight. Who would have thought that Sarah could bear a son to Abraham in their old age?

And surely he was a source of joy to them as he grew into a beautiful little boy. How his aged parents delighted in his soft baby hands and feet, his velvet skin, and then his every development: his first toothless smiles, his attempts to roll over, to sit up, his first unsteady steps. How they loved his every move, and how his mother relished holding, feeding and nurturing him. Happily she breast-fed him until it was evident that he was able to manage other food. Almost regretfully she had to accept it was time to wean him.

There was only one flaw in the happiness of those days. Ishmael did not share their joy, understandably resenting the intrusion of this baby into the territory that up to now had been exclusively his. He wasted no opportunity to behave spitefully to his little half-brother and smouldered with jealousy, so that there was no reasoning with him.

When it was time to wean Isaac, Abraham decided to throw a feast for him. As he carefully selected the fatted calf, he reflected on the day, probably at least two years ago now, when he had hurriedly prepared a meal for those unexpected guests who had foretold the birth of his son. He chuckled when he thought of Sarah's astonished face and her unbelieving laughter. Now they were truly laughing for joy.

He called Ishmael to come over and help him as he killed the calf. The well-built boy, now 13 or 14 years old, hauled the carcass onto his shoulders with ease and carried it off to be butchered. After a few minutes he reappeared and Abraham watched him as he swung by, loose-limbed and whistling. Nearby, Isaac was sitting in the dust playing with some roughly carved toys. His face lit up as he saw Ishmael coming. He scrambled up, calling, 'Ithmael! Ithmael!' in his baby lisping voice. Ishmael glanced down and a malicious expression crossed his face. He kicked the baby's game to pieces, leaving him to wail disconsolately.

Abraham frowned. It was not the first time he had seen Ishmael behave meanly to his small half-brother. He guessed that an insecure and jealous heart throbbed under that rough camel-skin coat. Sarah had seen the incident too and ran to her baby. She picked him up and cuddled him, meanwhile venting her indignation on the retreating form of Ishmael. Abraham sighed. He hated this discord in his family.

Later that evening he put his hand on Ishmael's shoulder and attempted to reason with him.

'Ishmael, son!' The boy flinched. Abraham ploughed on. 'There is no need for you to behave unkindly to Isaac. You have been my son for many years. You are still my son!'

Ishmael shook off the fatherly hand. 'But I'm not your heir,' he muttered. 'I don't matter to you any more. It is Isaac whom you really love!'

Abraham looked at him sadly. It was true that this wild donkey of a son was not so lovable as Isaac. Nevertheless, he was his own flesh and blood, and he did love him and wanted to care for him. This tension was a source of grief to him.

Sarah had been aware right from the start of Ishmael's antagonism, and had kept a wary eye on him. If she had hoped that he would be a loving and protective elder brother, she was disappointed. Instead there had been the mean little jibes, the resentful looks, the spiteful pinches and prods, when he thought no one was watching. He seemed to despise the little boy and delight in making him cry. Then he would taunt him, 'Laughing boy, laughing boy! Who is laughing now then? You should be called cry baby, not

Isaac!' Sarah was dismayed, but as time went on, dismay began to turn to anger. Sometimes she was afraid that Ishmael's increasing cruelty would result in permanent harm. He was so unpredictable and wild. He did not know what to do with this raging jealousy, the pain of being overlooked. He who had been the only heir for 13 years was now nobody! He lived with the strange anomaly that he was indeed the elder brother, but was not regarded as the 'firstborn'. It was hard, but his reaction of anger and cruelty could not be tolerated.

Things came to a head on the day of the feast. Everything was going so well! The food was delicious, and all the guests were having a wonderful time. Isaac was the centre of attention – people had come from miles around to see this miracle baby who had been born to such aged parents. Some of them had brought gifts, and the curly-headed toddler was happily playing with a new toy under a tree as Abraham rose to make a speech. All eyes except Sarah's were on Abraham. She kept a constant maternal eye on Isaac.

Ishmael was lurking in the shadows and sidled towards the little boy. Suddenly he snatched the new toy from Isaac and held it over his head out of reach. The child grabbed for it, but Ishmael held it tantalisingly beyond him, then ran off. Isaac stumbled after him, and Ishmael stopped and made as if to give it back, then at the last moment swung it away again. This went on for some minutes until Isaac gave up, exhausted, and sat down crying in the dust. Ishmael marched up and threw down the now-broken toy in disgust. 'Cry baby!' he sneered and pinched the child's leg hard.

Not many people had been aware of this by-play except Sarah. But now all eyes turned in that direction as they heard Isaac's cries. Exasperated, Sarah hurried over, scooped up Isaac, and confronted Ishmael. This was not the time or place for a show-down, so she simply ordered him to go to his tent. For a moment he stared at her mutinously and she thought he was about to defy her in front of all the guests. Then Hagar stalked up. She glared furiously at Sarah, grabbed Ishmael's hand, then turned on her heel and walked off with him.

It was an awkward moment. Abraham smoothed things over, and the party continued, but now a shadow was cast over it. Soon the guests began to take their leave, and Abraham and Sarah were left looking at each other. Sarah sat down wearily on a bench as the servants began to clear up around them. Isaac snuggled up to her on her lap, tired by the events of the long day. Abraham sat down by her and stroked Isaac's head. 'They will have to go, you know,' Sarah said with finality. 'We can't go on like this any more.'

Abraham was distressed. 'But where can they go? We can't just throw them out!'

'I don't know!' Sarah replied. 'I just know it will never work. These two boys cannot live together. Isaac is your heir and Ishmael cannot share his inheritance. You must send him and Hagar away!' She got up and carried the sleepy Isaac off to bed.

Abraham sat on, dejected, as the shadows lengthened, turning the dilemma over and over in his mind.

'He is my son!' he thought, thinking of Ishmael. 'I have fathered him, cared for him. I love him! I cannot drive him away.' But then he thought of Isaac. 'He also is my son and my heir. He is being continually subjected to Ishmael's cruel behaviour. I can't let it go on!' He thought of his wife and her efforts in the past to love Ishmael, and her frustration with his and Hagar's antagonism. He thought of Hagar, sad that he had used her to bear him a son and that, ever since, she had been a misfit in the household, her position exacerbated by the arrival of Isaac. He felt obligated to her, and her presence was a constant reminder of guilt. It was hard living with guilt, but it was harder to push her away! Things had reached an impasse. 'Oh, what shall I do?' he groaned.

The evening grew quiet around him; the debris from the feast was cleared away and he was alone. He turned his heart towards the Lord. Would El Shaddai speak to him and give him guidance? He sat, quietly waiting. In the stillness, the voice that had become familiar to him over the years spoke gently: 'Do not be distressed, Abraham. This time you must listen to Sarah your wife. She is right to say that Isaac is your heir; it is through him that this new nation will come. Don't worry about Ishmael. I will look after him, and also bring a nation about through him, because he also is your son.'

God had spoken. Abraham knew what he must do: he must listen to Sarah. This seemed strange since listening to her had not always been that helpful! In fact it was because of listening to her that they were now in this fix. But the voice was so clear and insistent that he had to obey. After a while he went to find Sarah.

She was sitting beside a sleeping Isaac, rocking him gently, but her mind was busy with the problem of Ishmael and Hagar. She longed to be rid of them. She longed for a peaceful existence, without conflict, without the constant reminder of their past inability to produce children and their pathetic human attempts to make God's plan work. If only she had trusted God instead of trying to manipulate people and events, they would not be faced with this dilemma now. But she had not trusted God. Instead she had given in to her selfish impatience, pushed her husband into sin, and the result was Ishmael. Ishmael had not brought peace, but trouble. How could they be free?

She turned as Abraham came in. In his face she saw a mixture of peace and pain, and she went to him. He took her hands and said quietly, 'You are right, Sarah. This cannot go on. Isaac is my heir, and I must send Hagar and Ishmael away.' She was conscious of a surge of relief – it would soon be over! But with it she was aware that this was costing Abraham. He was suffering at the thought of sending away the boy he had loved and may never see again. She pressed close to him, and stroked his face with her finger. 'Thank you' was all she could say.

Very early in the morning, Abraham got up and went out. Only Sarah was watching as three figures met in the misty dew under the oak tree. They embraced, and Abraham settled a large water skin on Ishmael's broad shoulder, and gave a bundle of food and clothes to Hagar. The little group stood together for a moment, then parted – the mother and son starting off on a long trail, and the father watching until they were visible no more.

*   *   *

What a sad and poignant story. Why did Abraham have to deal so ruthlessly, so uncompromisingly, with Hagar and Ishmael? We do not know, apart from the fact that it had to do with Isaac's inheritance. Yet many centuries later, Paul the apostle was able to draw upon this historical event to illustrate to the wayward Galatians the difference between being slave children of law and free children of grace. It seems that right back as far as Abraham and Sarah God foresaw the need to lay down a principle in dealing with this important issue.

The Galatians had heard the gospel from Paul and received it with joy. They were pagan Gentiles with no obligation to obey the Old Testament Law. They had believed in Jesus as the only mediator between God and humankind, and joyfully received forgiveness of sins; they were accepted by God because of the blood of Jesus. Paul eventually moved on to other towns, where he also preached the gospel, but in his wake came a group of zealous Jews who preached a mixed message.

These Judaisers came into town and told the joyful new converts that simply believing in Jesus was not enough. In order to please God, they must add to their salvation works of the law, they must be circumcised and observe certain days and rituals. In no time their precious freedom had been replaced by an anxious, meticulous regime of rule-keeping. They were bound in a tight net of legalism.

Paul was not just annoyed; he was enraged! As quickly as he could he dashed off an epistle by the next mail, the words pouring out of his quill, scorching the parchment. 'You foolish Galatians! Who has bewitched you?' he fulminated. 'A man is not justified by observing the law, but by faith in Jesus Christ' (Galatians 2:16). He went on to say that if justification by the law were possible, he would have qualified, as he was the most zealous law-keeper who ever breathed! But he was found to be a sinner and only Jesus was able to save him. He had died to the law that he might live to God. By trying to live by the law, these Galatians were nullifying the grace of God, 'for if righteousness could be gained through the law, Christ died for nothing' (2:21).

A deep urgency characterises this epistle. Paul is desperate for the Galatians to get the point that slavish obedience to a set of rules is not just unnecessary, it is flying in the face of God's amazing grace. It is saying that Jesus' death was not an adequate sacrifice and must be supplemented by some human effort. Paul dared not let this terrible misunderstanding continue to circulate, as it would cripple the gospel's power, and the spread of Christianity could have ended right there.

To illustrate, he appealed to the story of Abraham casting out Hagar and Ishmael: 'for it is written that Abraham had two sons, one by the slave woman and the other by the free

woman. His son by the slave woman was born in the ordinary way; but his son by the free woman was born as the
result of a promise' (4:22–23). He goes on to say that, figuratively speaking, these two women represent two covenants.
Hagar stands for Mount Sinai, where the Mosaic Law was
given, and all her children are slaves. In other words all who
live under the law are slaves to it. In case they don't get the
point, Paul drives it home by saying that Mount Sinai is like
the present city of Jerusalem, the centre of Jewish festivals,
rituals and law-keeping, and that all in that system are slaves!

But now, he says, we (i.e. Christians) have a different
mother. We are not born of the slave woman, Hagar. Sarah,
the free woman, is our mother. We have had supernatural
birth. We don't have to have anything to do with the head-
quarters of Judaism. We don't have to adhere to that system,
because we belong to a new Jerusalem. We are like Isaac, the
child of the promise. We are born from above, supernaturally.

Then he says an interesting thing. He says that the son of
the slave woman 'persecuted the son born by the power of
the Spirit' (4:29). When Ishmael behaved cruelly to Isaac, it
seems that he set something of a precedent. Ever since that
time, there has been conflict between those who walk by the
works of the law and those who live by the Spirit. Paul goes
so far as to use the word 'persecute'. Often, those who live
gloriously free from the entanglements of the law arouse
jealousy and outrage in legalists. The pride that entered the
heart of the human race at the Fall in the Garden of Eden
will not allow humanity to believe that all their efforts to
please God and win a place in heaven are totally inadequate.
The message of the cross is foolishness to them. They must
be able to secure a place by working very hard to be holy by
obeying rules.

With hindsight we can look back to those days and understand Paul's urgency to bring clarity. If he did not set out

clearly from the beginning the true nature of Christianity, its uniqueness to bestow salvation would be lost. Christianity would simply decline into an obscure sect within Judaism. Nothing would have changed; the Law would still be deemed the only means of pleasing God.

Of course this does not only apply to those Galatians. Christianity has been plagued throughout its history by distortions of the gospel that are all variations on the same theme. In the first century it was the demand for circumcision, while in the Middle Ages in Europe it was penance and buying indulgences and wearing hairshirts. Now in the twenty-first century, many still impose rules upon themselves in an effort to make themselves acceptable to God. Some believers will say that they are saved through the blood of Jesus, that they are cleansed and forgiven, but if they drink a glass of wine or wear ear-rings, or if a man wears his hair long, they think they will lose their salvation.

Works of the law force attention back to the individual: How am I doing? Am I holy enough? Am I making the grade? The accusing answer is always, 'No, you are not good enough. You are not doing enough. Try this, do more, cut out that . . . and perhaps you will make it.' That is the enemy's strategy: don't look at Jesus – look at yourself! He wants us to be preoccupied with our weaknesses and failings so we will give up in despair and never grow up as Christians. The opposite is what we must do: turn our eyes away from ourselves and look to Jesus – look at his sacrifice, his perfect life, his total obedience to the Father. Then all that wonderful righteousness becomes ours.

When we are preoccupied with him, rules like the length of our hair, what not to drink, whispering in church, not wearing make-up – all these and more – assume their right proportions. They are totally irrelevant.

Paul is not content with pointing out their silliness. He

shows us that we must be absolutely ruthless in throwing out legalism. We must not tolerate it. Why? Because legalism can never participate in inheriting the kingdom of God. Often it masquerades as holiness. It seems so appealing, so genuine, so impressive. But it is not the real thing. Real holiness is not about external acts; it is what has happened in our hearts. A clear distinction must be made.

Paul is so determined that nothing will compete with Jesus, because he alone can make us worthy of heaven. He was the 'seed', the firstborn of many brethren. He was the Isaac, the child of promise by supernatural birth. He had to go into the ground and die. By that act, he sowed his life like a seed to bring forth much fruit. We are also children of the promise. We are his inheritance, and we will inherit with him. Our inheritance owes nothing to our own efforts, but all to his life and death.

If that slave woman is still lurking around, don't be kind to her, do not give her an inch of space: she must go.

14

Isaac on the Altar

Sarah turned from Abraham and stumbled away blindly. Hardly aware of where she was, she came to the clump of oak trees, and leaned wearily against the trunk of the biggest one, her head on her arm. She stood thus for a while, shaking with shock, trying to get her pounding heart under control. Then, drained of all energy, she slid slowly down to the ground. She wished for oblivion to shut out the words she had just heard, but the tumult continued to whirl in her mind.

Her first reaction had been to ridicule what Abraham had said. He could not be serious! The very idea was ludicrous and not worth genuine consideration. 'Really, Abraham! What an absurd suggestion! Come on now, let's not mention it again. I wish you would not talk that way, even in jest.' But Abraham was not jesting. He was silent; then he tried again. 'Sarah, it's not as simple as that. I can't just forget it. Believe me, if it was just a mad idea of mine, I would! This is not something I want to do.' He sighed, stood up, paced about, came back and stood in front of her. This was so difficult! 'Sarah, this is from God.'

That was when she had exploded. Tremulous with anger, she stuttered, 'How could that possibly be from God? He would not command you to do such a terrible thing to your son! To Isaac!' Her voice rose to a crescendo. 'No, Abraham! No. You're wrong. It's a mistake. He didn't, couldn't have said that. Please, Abraham, say it was a mistake! You didn't hear him say that!'

He tried to put his arm around her shaking shoulders, draw her close, but she stood stiff, staring up at him with terrified eyes.

The cruel gods of the surrounding Canaanites apparently demanded such things. She remembered back to the days in Ur how the Chaldees sought to appease the capricious deities whom they worshipped with ritual infant sacrifice. 'But our God is not like that,' she whispered. 'He is different . . . isn't he?'

'I can only tell you what I know,' Abraham persisted quietly. 'Our God is awesome, but not cruel and brutal. When he speaks, there is a sort of fear, but it is not oppressive and crushing. How many years ago is it since I first heard that voice, Sarah? Do you remember when I told you that he was telling me to leave Ur? And then Haran? And the many times since? Do you think I don't know that voice by now?'

She nodded dumbly, her face white. He went on, 'And what about the promises? Have they not come true?'

'But that's just the point!' she flashed back, her fists pounding his chest. 'Isaac is the promised child, so how can God want you to sacrifice the very one he gave? It doesn't make sense. All the other promises about being the founder of a new nation are wrapped up in him. No, no . . .' She dissolved into heart-rending sobs. Again he reached to her and held her. He understood, for he had been telling himself the same things. It was totally illogical. But it was so far away from his own thinking that he knew it could not have originated from himself. He knew the voice of God by now, but

had he been mistaken? Had he heard it correctly? He wished
there was some doubt, but it had been so clear, so unmistak-
ably overwhelmingly clear, that he was certain. God had
said, 'Take your son, Isaac, whom you love, and go to
Moriah. Sacrifice him as an offering to me on the mountain.'

'Sarah, I can only say to you that I believe it was God who
spoke to me. I believe that he gave Isaac to us, but he is not
ours to possess. God has a huge, wide purpose in his life.
Somehow – I don't know how – he will still accomplish it.'

She had struggled in his arms and pushed him away.
Shocked and amazed, she had stumbled over to the oak tree.
Now here she was, on the ground, heavy with grief, while
tears slowly trickled down her tired old face.

She was still there late in the afternoon. The first shock
had died down, leaving her numb. She became aware that the
tree roots were digging into her, so now she turned on her
back and watched the waving branches. It was under this
very tree that the three strangers had sat and eaten roast
lamb. Then, calling for Sarah, one of them had declared that
she would have a son by this time next year. She remembered
now how she had laughed incredulously, and been gently
rebuked.

She recalled now the sense of awe that had overwhelmed
her and how, realising that it was God himself who had
spoken, she had come to a place of faith that had enabled
her to conceive the promised child. That had been a year of
purest joy. She had entered into a new dimension of peace
and fellowship with God and carried her baby with a light
heart. Yes, God had seemed very close, and the day of Isaac's
birth was the happiest day of her life. So why this strange
command that her husband thought he had heard?

But she knew her Abraham well enough by now to know
that if God spoke, he would obey him. He would not be
deflected by her sorrow, anger or lack of understanding.

There was not much time to get used to the situation. Early the next morning, she heard the sound of wood being chopped. When she emerged from her tent, Eliezer was tying faggots in bundles, and Isaac was hopping about in high excitement. When he saw her, he ran to her shouting, 'Mother! I am going with Father. We are going on a journey together.' Her heart lurched at the sight of his eager young face.

Abraham came over. 'Son, go and fetch your things,' he said, and turned to Sarah as the boy ran off.

'You are going then?' she queried unnecessarily.

He put his arms round her. 'I must,' he whispered into her hair. Then he held her away from him and looked into her bewildered face, and tenderness swept over him. She had followed him faithfully, through good times and bad, through deserts and watered plains, famine and plenty. He had endangered her life and her virtue more than once, but together they had believed God and brought forth the promised heir. How could he do this to her? How could he do it to himself? Why was he doing it at all?

'I must,' he repeated. 'You know I have always sought to obey God. I will not be disobedient now, even though I do not understand. Sarah, while I am away, ponder the character and the words of God. Has he ever let us down? Let us trust him now!' Thus he tried to encourage her, even though his own heart was full of pain.

Isaac came up, leading a donkey. He was carrying a small bundle wrapped in a cloth, which he proceeded to tie onto the back of the donkey.

'Time to go!' said Abraham with a heartiness he did not feel. 'Say goodbye to your mother, son.'

Isaac was as tall as Sarah now. He put his muscular young arms around her and hugged her, surprised at her passionate kisses and the tears in her eyes. 'Mother!' he laughed.

'We'll only be gone for a few days. Don't worry about us. We'll be fine.' Eager to be gone, he grabbed the rope around the donkey's neck, and tugged his father's sleeve.

So the little group set out: Abraham, Isaac and two servants, and two donkeys, which carried their water, provisions and blankets.

Shading her eyes, Sarah watched them for a long time as they wound down the hillside to the valley. They were long out of sight before she finally turned and went back to the campsite. Would she ever see her son again? As she went, she made some calculations. Moriah was about three days' journey away. Three days there, three back . . . and however long in between for whatever took place there. She had perhaps a week to wait, think, agonise and pray.

She spent most of that week at that spot overlooking the trail down which Abraham and Isaac had disappeared. As she crouched there under the oak trees, she turned over and over in her mind the promises about Isaac. After the long, hopeless, barren years, she had found it hard at first to receive faith to conceive, but the word of God had worked like yeast in her heart, growing and swelling, until her body, mind and spirit were permeated with life, and her whole being shouted, 'Yes! I believe!' Then to act and conceive was just a natural outworking of faith.

When she cradled her new-born son in her arms, she could have confidently told anyone that the will of God is good, perfect and acceptable – the promised son had come! But there were other promises wrapped up in him: he was to be the forerunner of a new nation. So how could God now demand his life as a sacrifice? How could that be acceptable? Did he not intend to keep those promises? Did God keep some promises and not others? In which case how could anyone trust him, if they never knew which ones he intended to keep and which ones to let go? Despairing, she turned this

conundrum over and over in her mind, unable to get past it.
She did not want to sink back into the treacherous swamps
of unbelief after years of standing on solid ground.

He appeared to be demanding the death of this son. Or
was he? Was it really him, or some aberration in Abraham's
brain? After all, he was very old . . . Then furiously her
thoughts rushed on to the stark, terrible deed that must be
enacted if it truly was the will of God. Not only would she
have to face the sorrow of bereavement, and bereavement
caused by a violent death, but, worst of all, bereavement
caused by the hand of her beloved husband.

One day during that agonising wait, she came back to the
word that had originally germinated faith in her unbelieving
heart: 'Is anything too hard for the Lord?' She had gone
through the unimaginable experience of carrying a child in
her womb and bringing him forth in her ninetieth year. How
had she done that? Through the power of El Shaddai, the
Lord Almighty. It had not been too hard for him. Abraham's
body and her own had been as good as dead, as far as func-
tions of reproduction were concerned. But, amazingly, life
had sprung out of apparent death!

She had been lounging back against the trunk of the tree,
but now sat bolt upright, her body and mind taut with con-
centration, as if to focus on something distant that she
strained to catch, to see, to hear . . . She knew El Shaddai was
the creator God – he had created the heavens and the earth,
and he had created Isaac in a dead womb – but could he *re-
create*? Could he bring something, or more specifically
someone, out of death into new life? Her breath seemed
stuck in her throat as she grappled with this enormous new
thought. Could she dare to believe that this was his plan?

It was too big, too overwhelming a thought for her to
comprehend. Stiffly she rose to her feet and looked out over
the hills and plains towards Mount Moriah. Would her

husband really take a knife and plunge it into their son? Could he? And if he did, what would happen next? Would she ever see Isaac striding back along that path?

Suddenly she flung her arms up in a gesture of abandonment. The Lord had given Isaac; the Lord could take him away. If he wanted to, he could bring him back. But whatever he decided, he would do and she had no control over it. It would be better to stop fighting, and acquiesce, surrender to that will that seemed so terrifying from her point of view, but was perhaps wonderful when seen from his perspective. 'It's all yours anyway,' she murmured. 'These hills and valleys – everything, especially Isaac. You are great and mighty. There is nothing I would withhold from you – even my son.'

Peace stole into her heart. She had a vague feeling that something cosmic was taking place, but it was all too undefined and distant to make sense of. She wandered back to her tent and slept.

Three days later, Sarah was watching from the ridge, shading her eyes with her hand against the glaring sun. She thought she saw a movement out there on the rocky trail. Gradually the little group came more into view, and she could see the donkeys and several people. But how many? She waited anxiously. The group came on, sometimes disappearing from sight as they went round rocks and clumps of bushes, but all the while getting nearer and nearer. At length, they were plainly visible: a donkey with a man riding on it, and another donkey behind, and two people walking along beside. She thought there was someone on the second donkey. Then suddenly the figure slid off and came running towards her. 'Mother! Mother!' She opened her arms and the lithe, happy boy ran into them – Isaac, laughing as usual, and very much alive!

It was some time before the joyous emotion of reunion

subsided enough for Abraham to sit quietly with Sarah and
tell her all that he and Isaac had been through. He began to
recount not only the journey but the tangled thought pro-
cesses and his eventual obedience and deliverance.

As he recounted it, she could picture it all: the arduous
climb up the bare rocky mountain in the heat; the old man,
a sharp knife tucked into his belt, carrying the brass pot
swinging from its chain full of smouldering charcoal; the
vigorous young man sweating under the prickly load of fire-
wood on his back. Wood; fire; knife: the implements of sacrifice. Isaac had often been with his father when he was
selecting an unblemished lamb for sacrifice, so he knew the
signs. She could picture them toiling up the track and anticipated the question before Abraham came to it.

'We had gone quite a long way,' he was saying, 'and I could
tell he was puzzled. But we kept walking. It's quite a climb,
you know, and we didn't have much breath left for talking!
He had gone on ahead and I came round a boulder and
found him waiting for me . . .' Abraham was silent for a few
minutes, struggling with the emotions that the memory
evoked. He took a deep breath and Sarah held his hand
tightly. 'He said, "Father, we have brought wood and fire for
a burnt offering, but where is the lamb?"' Abraham's voice
cracked slightly as he said the last word.

'Sarah, what could I say? I looked at his beautiful young
face, so innocent, so trusting. How could I say, "You are the
lamb"? It was as if all my questions and thoughts of the last
three days were suddenly focused. You see, I had had three
days with him – three wonderful days as we camped out
under the stars and laughed together and had such fun as
father and son. Never had my love for him been so strong.
Never had I enjoyed him more than on those three days
together. I tell you, my heart was breaking as we ascended
that mountain.'

They were both crying now. Sarah could hardly bear to imagine the conflict of pleasure and pain, joy and agony, that had wrestled in her husband's heart. She wiped her cheek and whispered, 'What did you say?'

Again a long pause as Abraham sought to find words to communicate. He was looking over the familiar landscape, but in his mind's eye he was seeing the trusting face of his son and hearing the unchanging inexorable voice of God: 'Go from Ur . . . Leave your land and kindred . . . I will make of you a nation . . . You will have a son . . . Your descendants shall be as the sand on the seashore . . . Sarah will have a son called Isaac . . . he will be the first of a great nation . . . Go take your son Isaac, whom you love . . .'

'It has been God all along,' he said, and felt the words sounded trite. He tried again: 'He always had a purpose, but he could only tell me a bit at a time. I think I suddenly realised that this idea of a sacrifice was not a new and sudden thing; he had always intended it, just as he had always intended to have a nation. His plans have never changed, but I had to change as each bit unfolded. Somehow I knew that there had to be a sacrifice, but I could trust him when the time came. So I just said, "God will provide the lamb, my son." He seemed to be content with that.'

Sarah tried to digest this. 'But what about when you reached the top?'

Abraham smiled slightly. 'He was so helpful! He ran around and found stones to build an altar with and helped me put the wood on top. We were pretty tired from the long walk and sat down to rest and eat. But I could see him looking around all the time for the lamb. I . . .' Tears threatened again, but he persisted. 'I . . . we . . . went over to the altar. I tied him and somehow got him on top. I pulled out my knife. I was about to strike . . . lifted the knife . . . suddenly a voice, God's voice; "Don't do it, Abraham!" I dropped the knife.' He let out his breath with a gasp. Sarah clung to him weakly.

'Do you know, Sarah, another wonderful thing happened then. Suddenly there was a ram there, caught by its horns in a bush. So I sacrificed that instead. God did provide a lamb.'

She nodded wordlessly. Dimly she saw that two loves had comfortably lived side by side in his heart until now, but one had had to give way to the other. Love for God must reign, for it controls and purifies all other loves. How hard it was to make that choice, but how strong Abraham had been! She was amazed at him, and loved him afresh. She almost missed what he said next, slowly and humbly, in a low voice: 'I think God was pleased, because he said, "Do not harm the lad, for now I know that you fear God since you have not withheld your only son from me." And he went on to repeat all his promises. He said, "In your seed shall all the nations of the earth be blessed, because you have obeyed my voice."'

*　　*　　*

Abraham was a mighty man of vision, but surely neither he nor Sarah could have foreseen that centuries later, on that same mountain, Solomon's temple would one day stand in all its glory, and that where Abraham had built his simple altar, a great high altar would be the place of sacrifice of numerous sheep and lambs, slain as offerings for sin. Nor would they have foreseen that very near this same place, the blood would be shed of another son of promise – a sinless one who would offer up his life as a sacrifice to atone for sin, once and for all. He also went out to this place bearing wood on his shoulder. But though he cried in anguish, 'Father, let this cup pass from me!' there was no reprieve from heaven for him. The fire of judgement fell on him, the knife of a holy God tore into him and he who was called the Lamb of God was slain. But the promises of God did not fall to the ground, forgotten and unfulfilled. The seed of a new nation was in him, and though he fell into the ground, and died, resurrection life sprang forth. 'Before Abraham was born, I am,' he declared to a scandalised group of Pharisees. 'Abraham rejoiced at the thought of seeing my day; he saw it and was glad' (John 8:56, 58).

How much of that day did Abraham see? Enough to deliver up his son to death and receive him back, 'figuratively speaking' (Hebrews 11:19).

15

The Death of Sarah

Many years passed. The aged parents watched their son grow into adult manhood, but Sarah did not live to see her grandchildren. When Isaac was 40, Abraham sent his servant to Haran to find a wife for his son from among his own kindred, who were still settled there. The servant brought back a beautiful young woman called Rebekah, who became Isaac's wife and the mother of the next generation. She had twins, of whom one was to become Israel, the name of the new nation that was now in its infancy.

But Sarah never met Rebekah. She died at the age of 127, three years before her son's marriage. How did she die? We are not told the details – only that it was at Kiriath Arba, near Hebron, which was not very far from Mamre, where they had received the visitation of the three heavenly strangers under the oak tree.

Abraham mourned and wept for the loss of his wife. She had been a faithful companion through a long and eventful life, spanning perhaps 100 years. Well might he mourn for her, and deeply feel the sorrow of bereavement! Did he have any regrets as he sat beside her still body? Looking back over the vista of years behind them, how did he view their life together?

Ur was probably a distant, faded memory now, difficult to recall through the haze of passing years. The bustle and hubbub of the thronged streets frowned over by the towering ziggurat was so far removed from the rolling hills and plains of Canaan. Sarah had never developed her cultural aspirations, or learned the arts, or engaged in philosophical debate; she had left the fashionable set and their homage to the impassive stone god, Nannar.

*   *   *

Abraham remembered the day they had turned their backs resolutely on Ur, and smiled tenderly as he saw Sarah again in his mind's eye, straining for one last look at what they were leaving behind. He remembered the tears on her cheeks as he had helped her climb back onto her camel, her face turned bravely to a new horizon. He shook his head now, thinking of her beside him, looking forward to the future, as the city of Ur faded out of sight.

What future? They knew nothing! He could hold out no promises of a comfortable house in a pleasant location. He just knew they had to find Canaan. He recalled her puzzled sigh, and then how she had looked up at him and smiled and said, 'Where you go, I will go.' And so they had gone.

She had been kind to his father, to old Terah, on that journey. She had tried to make him comfortable in his tent on cold nights, and talked with him of people he used to know and tried to make their monotonous diet more appetising. She had sympathised with him when they reached Haran, and Abraham knew that she had welcomed the respite in their journey, with the fresh opportunities that Haran afforded. She had been in no hurry to move on. There were more people to talk to, goods to buy, things to see, and life became more settled for a while.

But it did not, could not, last. Why? Because there was

another claim on their lives; a more urgent priority called them. Always that insistent voice, calling them forward, teaching them not to settle, to keep moving, searching, believing in something more. Again he saw that flaming sunset and heard the words that had seared themselves into his brain: 'I will bless you and make you a blessing . . . in you shall all the nations of the earth be blessed . . . I will give you the land . . . your descendants will be as the sand on the seashore . . .'

That was what had kept them going, moving, travelling, hoping. Even in the long barren years, hoping against hope. His heart ached again as he heard once more her despairing tears, month by month, year by year. How she had longed, ached, to be a mother! How she had berated herself, despised herself, for being unable to produce an heir! He recalled how he had tried in vain to reassure her that she was beautiful, desirable, whether she had children or not, and that one day, they were sure to turn up.

And she *was* so beautiful. His dim eyes now gazed upon the still form on the bed in the gloom of the tent, so slight and thin now. And empty. She was not there. It was difficult to equate this shrouded, shrivelled little figure with the vibrant, glowing, energetic woman of the desert. Images flashed upon his inner eye of her carrying her waterpot with grace and ease, swinging it up on her shoulder as if it weighed no more than a feather; striding around among the sheep, calling her maids to her to help with the shearing; kneading dough, her bare arms strong and brown, glinting with sweat. He could see her now, combing her long dark hair, twisting it up and sighing as it tumbled down again around her shoulders.

No wonder Pharaoh himself had been so attracted to this handsome woman! She never did understand that it was not only her striking looks that were so appealing, but her animated personality, her strength of character, her confidence and elegance. Put her next to any other woman and they paled into the background. Yes, even Hagar . . .

He groaned and sighed, not wanting to recall that episode just yet. He wanted to dwell on the beauties of his Sarah, to recall her companionship, her partnership with him through thick and thin. How he missed her! His heart would surely break, he told himself.

They had been adventurous years that she had shared with him, sometimes tempestuous, but at times monotonous and uneventful. They had had their troubles: the famine that had driven them down to Egypt, his own lies and deception, which had nearly cost him Sarah herself; then Lot and his wife had caused them much anguish. And through it all, the continuous intervention of a God who kept speaking and got him back on course when he went off it.

The biggest mistake of all, of course, was when he allowed himself to be swayed by Sarah's despair and unbelief into taking matters into his own hands. She had grown older and older, as is the nature of things, and had become so depressed! He stood up now and went to the doorway. He was in sudden need of air, almost as if he were back in that suffocating time. He looked out now towards the hills in the distance where the oaks of Mamre still stood, too far to be visible. He gazed unseeingly, preoccupied with the memory of her frustration, her mood swings, her absorption with her aging body. He could hear her passionate, despairing tears as she tried to come to terms with the fact that it was too late. Her womb was dry, the fountain had ceased to flow. She was old, too old – for pleasure, or for bearing a child.

And Hagar was so available, so fertile, so young, so . . . so . . . *there*! It had seemed such a sensible option when Sarah had presented him with it, even though he always knew in his heart of hearts that it was not the way God was going to choose – had already chosen in fact – to bring about the promised heir. But instead of taking the responsible stance as head of his household, he had gone along with it, complied, let her talk him into it. If only he had made a better choice! If only they had never gone down into Egypt and taken Hagar into their home in the first place! If only he had taken authority in his home and said, 'No. As for me and my house, we will trust God!' If only . . .

Death was a time for regrets, he was finding. He regretted the departure of Ishmael. He wondered where he was and what had become of him. What had happened to Hagar after he had said his last goodbye that early morning?

Isaac came into view and saw his father hovering at the tent door. He came up, and the two men went in and sat down wordlessly by the body of the woman who had been pivotal in both their lives. Isaac caressed her face, grey and waxy, and covered it again with the gauzy shroud. They both wept.

Abraham fell to remembering how she had changed in those desert days from tempestuous despair to calm, clear confidence in the word of God. He had not dared tell her of the last visitation he had had when he had called God by a new name, El Shaddai, and God had called him his friend, because his friend had repeated the promise about the baby, with specific details – it would be born next year. He had not told her; she could not have coped. But then God himself had come with his angels and told her to her face.

He put up his hand to his face now, and Isaac was astonished to see his father's shoulders shake slightly as he chuckled quietly. Abraham was oblivious, lost in his memories. He could hear Sarah's incredulous shriek of laughter, loud and clear. How embarrassed he had been! But after that, she had been quiet and thoughtful for days. He could see she was turning something over and over in her mind. Gradually a peace seemed to envelop her. She seemed to acquire a quiet and gentle spirit, which was so refreshing after her sadness. In fact her old sparkle returned, and he thought her even more beautiful than before, because there was a lightness in her spirit, a joy. He thought it was because of that wonderful afternoon when God had spoken. She changed after that; that was the simple explanation.

She had always been an obedient wife, he thought. But submissive? Was that the same thing? He realised now that although she had always gone along with him, there had to come a time when obedience sprang from her own heart, when she embraced the promises of God for herself. With that had come a change of attitude in all her relationships, but especially with him. She was now standing on God's word herself, not just being carried by her husband's faith.

Suddenly he realised that this had brought a deeper security to her, and in her security she could submit without fear. Their marriage took on a deeper joy. Once again Isaac was surprised when he looked up at his father, for although the tears were fresh upon his face, there was also a smile of pure happiness that curved the mouth under the white beard. Little did he know that the night of his own conception was now under review!

One by one others came in to sit with Abraham as he mourned: Eliezer, himself getting old now, maids, shepherds . . . They came and went and wept and reminisced, and they embraced Abraham and told him how they had loved Sarah and how they missed her now!

It was time to arrange her burial. A message had been sent to the leaders of the Hittites, who were the tribe occupying that part of the land at that time. A servant on lookout duty came and reported that a band of men was arriving. They approached, a long line of them winding up the slope. Abraham went out to greet them and chairs were brought and food and drink set before them.

At length, Abraham stood to his feet and addressed them: 'You know that I am a stranger and sojourner among you. Now I ask for a burial site among you that I can call my own in which to bury my dead.'

*   *   *

How strange! Abraham had been living among them for nearly three-quarters of a century, at least 60 or 70 years. He had grazed his cattle, no doubt traded goods, acquired servants, and lived his nomadic lifestyle all this time, yet still regarded himself as a stranger! The word that Abraham used described a resident alien with some footing in the community but restricted rights.

Later in the New Testament, the writer to the Hebrews also describes Abraham as 'a stranger in a foreign country' (11:9). He left Ur, he left Haran, he had been in Canaan for decades, but it seems as if he never really came home! He 'sojourned' there, as the King James version says – an old-fashioned word, which conveys the sense of living temporarily in a place. But was not this the land promised to him and his descendants? Could he not have claimed it as his home?

He knew it was not yet his. He was one who by faith and patience inherited the promise. He was confident that the time would come, though not in his own lifetime, when Canaan would be the possession of the new nation that God had planted in Isaac. In the meantime, he wanted a tiny plot, a foothold that was like a guarantee. He wanted to lay the bones of his wife there, and eventually his own bones, as a testimony – a declaration of faith that in the fullness of time the promise would be completely accomplished. This faith was handed down to his real children: those who would come after him who would also live by faith, such as the apostle Paul, who would write, 'For we know in part . . . but when perfection comes, the imperfect disappears' (1

Corinthians 13:9–10). In the meantime we live with the imperfect, believing in the coming of the perfect!

*　　*　　*

The sons of Heth, the Hittites, looked at each other. They knew this man! He had been among them for years. He was a man of solid worth – not a lightweight nobody. They had observed him; they appreciated him; they had watched his life and seen his conduct. They were open to giving him a stake in their land because they were not afraid that he would abuse it. He had shown that he was not greedy.

'You are a mighty prince,' they said. 'You may bury your dead wherever you wish. Take your pick!'

Then Abraham rose again in his place and bowed to them respectfully. 'May I then have your permission to approach Ephron, the son of Zohar? I would like to buy his field in which is a cave.' Ephron was sitting among the Hittites and he jumped up and exclaimed impulsively, 'No, my lord! I would be happy to give you the field. I would be honoured if you would accept it from me.'

Abraham smiled gratefully at him, and bowed. Very respectfully he said, 'Please listen to me: I will pay the full price for the field. Please accept it from me that I may bury my wife there.'

Ephron glanced around at his fellow elders. They were nodding, signalling that this was the right way to negotiate. Ephron turned back to Abraham and said, 'My lord, I will take a price of 400 shekels. Let not this stand in your way! Please – bury your dead!'

Abraham was satisfied. It was a fair price. He called Eliezer to him and at length he returned with the silver. Solemnly he weighed out 400 shekels. It was now recognised that Ephron's field, with its trees and borders, was officially Abraham's property.

The meeting broke up and the Hittite clan departed. Abraham went once more to stand by his beloved Sarah. He was glad that he had bought a resting place for her bones. She had learned to love this land and had shared with him the belief that their offspring would populate it. She would have understood. She would have rejoiced that they had a tangible foothold in the inheritance they had lived for but never received.

In the mellow light of the afternoon, the procession set off. Eliezer and Isaac and a couple of sturdy servants hoisted the bier with its shrouded burden onto their shoulders. Abraham followed and the rest of his company – shepherds, menservants and maidservants – straggled along behind. Slowly they wound along the ridge and descended the valley, then up again and over the rocky terrain until they came to the field near Mamre – the place that held so many memories. The light was fading now, but Abraham could see the altar he had built there many years ago as a pledge of his faith in an unfailing God. It was fitting.

As the sunset flamed across the evening sky, they buried Sarah in the cave and sealed the entrance. Abraham knew that the next time it was opened would be to receive his bones. He was content. She had gone now: the woman of faith who had died in faith, not having received all the promises, but having seen them from afar, and having welcomed them. She was one of the heroes of faith who 'were longing for a better country – a heavenly one. Therefore God is not ashamed to be called their God, for he has prepared a city for them.'[1]

Abraham turned his face to the glorious sky. Was she even now entering that city?

---

[1] Hebrews 11:16.

Study Guide

Chapter 1: It All Began with Abraham

1. When Stephen was on trial for blasphemy, he started his speech in defence by reminding his hearers of Abraham, the founding father of the Israelite nation. Why is Abraham important to both Jews and Christians?
2. Read Romans 4:9–17. Who are the children of Abraham?

Chapter 2: Leaving Ur

Abraham and Sarah set out from Ur, a civilised city, and headed for the unknown, living in tents.
1. When Jesus called you to follow him, what equivalent to Ur did you leave behind?
2. Do you think you have adopted a pilgrim mentality?
3. Are you resistant to change?
4. Do you think you have settled for something less than the original vision?

Chapter 3: The Call

1. How did God call you to follow him?
2. How did you respond?

3. What else has he called you to?
4. What implications has it had for your relationships, e.g. with parents, spouse, friends?

Chapter 4: What Is a Call?

1. What are Christians called out from? (See Romans 12:1–2 and Galatians 1:4.)
2. What are they called into? (See 1 Corinthians 1:2,9.)
3. Read Isaiah 51:1–2. You, like Abraham, were called as an individual. He, however, did not remain as one. Are you aware that you are now part of this new nation? How does this affect you?
5. Are you enjoying playing your part in the body of Christ? (See 1 Corinthians 12:27.)

Chapter 5: Travelling to Canaan

1. Is there a sense of moving on in your spiritual journey?
2. How do you view promises that God has made to you? Are you in faith for their fulfilment?
3. Abraham built an altar as a statement that he had heard God and believed him. Are there any steps that you can take to demonstrate your trust in God while you wait to see the fulfilment of his word?

Chapter 6: The Desert

1. Can you recall a desert period in your life?
2. What feelings did you experience? (E.g. fear, frustration, panic, thirst.)
3. Were you tempted to wallow in self-pity? Give way to despair or anger? Anything else?
4. What did you discover about yourself? About God?

Chapter 7: Egypt

1. Have you ever been shocked to discover that someone whom you trusted and respected was capable of acting very selfishly? How did you react?
2. The Bible does not 'whitewash' its heroes. What characteristics that we see in Abraham and Sarah can we avoid? What things can we emulate?
3. What, in practice, does submission mean to you?
5. Can you extend forgiveness to a partner who has let you down?

Chapter 8: Hagar

1. Sarah was well past child-bearing years. How do you feel about growing old?
2. Have you been tempted to 'push' the work of God along by employing less than pure means?
3. Does the end ever justify the means?
4 Is your personal fulfilment more important to you than the will of God?

Chapter 9: The God Who Sees

1. How does the knowledge that God is watching over you affect you? Does it comfort you or scare you?
2. If you are a victim of cruelty or injustice, does the knowledge that 'God sees' change anything for you?

Chapter 10: A New Name

1. Abraham and Sarah were given new names by God. Read Isaiah 62:3–4 and Isaiah 61:3. How has God changed you? What would be an appropriate new name for you?

2. Read Colossians 2:6–23. Think carefully about anything that has become an empty ritual in your life. Are you relying upon the outward observance of some rite to find favour with God? Under the New Covenant we are free from rules and rituals, e.g. to do with eating, drinking, special days, festivals, etc. Do not let anyone hinder your liberty!

Chapter 11: The Visitation

1. Read Hebrews 11. Faith pleases God. What have you received by faith?
2. Verse 10 says that Abraham went 'looking for a city' (NASB). What are you looking for?
3. What words has God spoken to you that have stimulated faith?
4. Does age have anything to do with receiving God's promises?

Chapter 12: The Abimelech Episode

1. Read 1 Peter 3. Verse 6 talks about submission without fear. How does this work out in your life? Is your life one of constant yielding to God, or is it a continual tug-of-war?
2. How can we cultivate a gentle and quiet spirit? Do we want to cultivate it?
3. What is your attitude to your body? Do you hate it? Neglect it? Or are you obsessed with it? Can you accept that God wants to dwell in it by his Spirit? (Read 1 Corinthians 6:12–20.)

Chapter 13: Isaac Comes, Ishmael Goes

1. Abraham was told to listen to his wife. Are you a good listener to your spouse? To other people in your life?

2. Read Galatians 4. Who do Hagar and Sarah represent in Paul's analogy?
3. In the context of the present day, what do you understand about being 'under the law'?
4. Why is Paul so insistent that we are clear about being emancipated from the law?

Chapter 14: Isaac on the Altar

1. Are there people or things in your life, other than the Lord himself, that take first place? Have you ever been tested on this point?
2. It is breathtaking to see how this amazing story prophetically portrays God's plan to sacrifice his Son. What details parallel the crucifixion of Jesus?
3. Read Isaiah 53, another prophetic passage pointing forward to the substitutionary death of Jesus. God provided the Lamb! Have you ever thanked him for his amazing plan of salvation?

Chapter 15: The Death of Sarah

1. Read Hebrews 12:1–2. Sarah was one of a 'great cloud of witnesses' who ran the race of faith. How would you like to be remembered?
2. Hebrews 11:39 says that they 'were all commended for their faith'. Look through the chapter and see how other heroes expressed their faith. How can we be encouraged by their example?
3. What do you consider to be the 'something better' (v. 40) that God has planned for us?

Bibliography

John Calvin, *Genesis*, The Geneva series of commentaries.
Victor P. Hamilton, *The Book of Genesis*, New International Commentary on the Old Testament.
Derek Kidner, *Genesis*, Tyndale Old Testament Commentaries.
F. B. Meyer, *Abraham, Friend of God* (Ambassador, 1993).
Andrew Murray, *The Holiest of All* (Baker, 1997).
Arthur Pink, *Gleanings in Genesis* (Moody, 1995).
The Times Atlas of the Bible (Collins, 2000).
F. F. Bruce, *Places They Knew* (S.U., 1984).

Index of Life Issues

Page numbers often mark the beginning of a topic that continues for several pages.

Abraham: Friend of God

by Cleland Thom

Abraham means 'the father is exalted'. Far from perfect, he nevertheless found favour with God and miraculously became the father of a child, a nation and a faith. Through it all he discovered the secret of becoming a friend of God.

Let Abraham's story remind you of what it is to be a friend of God – someone with whom God can share his own heart.

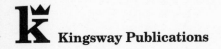
Kingsway Publications

Mary: the Mother of Jesus

by Wendy Virgo

From the first Christmas to the first Easter and beyond, we follow Mary, the mother of Jesus.

Wendy Virgo's skilful and moving narrative brings to life the dilemmas and dangers, the price and the pain, of being mother to the most special Person in history.

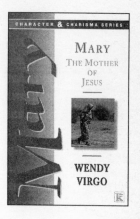

 Kingsway Publications